# Scientology Step by Step

## Understanding the Beliefs, Practices & Goals of Scientology

Michael Chase

# PREFACE

Welcome to *Scientology Step by Step – Understanding the Beliefs, Practices & Goals of Scientology*. This book was created as a clear and accessible guide for those interested in understanding Scientology's unique approach to spirituality, self-discovery, and personal development. Whether you're completely new to Scientology, have a casual curiosity, or even possess a more detailed interest, this book aims to give you a well-rounded, honest, and straightforward overview of what Scientology is all about.

Scientology can be a topic surrounded by a lot of intrigue and sometimes mystery, and that's partly because its beliefs, language, and practices may feel unfamiliar at first. Terms like "Thetan," "E-Meter," "Engram," and "Clear" might sound unfamiliar to you, but as you explore these pages, they'll start to make sense and reveal their significance. This book takes a step-by-step approach to introducing these terms and ideas to make them accessible and relatable, regardless of your background.

The foundation of Scientology lies in the belief that each of us is a spiritual being with unlimited potential, and the journey to fully realize that potential is called "The Bridge to Total Freedom." In this book, we explore what it means to walk that Bridge, how Scientologists believe they can overcome the limitations of the mind and the body, and ultimately, how they aim to reach a state of spiritual freedom. Along the way, we'll uncover the practices that define Scientology, from its fundamental ideas about the mind to its methods of self-reflection and improvement through auditing and training.

The first chapter introduces you to the origins of Scientology and its founder, L. Ron Hubbard, providing historical context for the movement. From there, we go into the concept of the Thetan, a central element of Scientology that describes the spiritual essence believed to exist within each of us. The early chapters are dedicated to explaining these foundational concepts that shape how Scientologists view themselves and the world around them.

One of the most unique aspects of Scientology is its structured framework, known as "The Dynamics of Existence." This framework encourages individuals to view their lives in relation to various areas—such as personal well-being, family, community, and even humankind as a whole. The idea is that each of us exists within and influences these dynamics, and understanding this interconnectedness is essential to personal growth. As you progress through the chapters, you'll find detailed explanations of how these dynamics shape the Scientologist's worldview.

Another major focus of this book is "The Bridge to Total Freedom," a structured path that serves as a roadmap for spiritual progression in Scientology. This path includes various stages and states, from initial discovery to reaching a state known as "Clear." We'll explore each of these stages in depth, looking at how Scientologists view their progress along this path and what they hope to achieve with each step.

The book also covers auditing—a central practice in Scientology aimed at helping individuals confront and resolve negative experiences, often called "engrams," which are believed to limit personal growth. Auditing sessions, typically done with the assistance of an "auditor" and the use of a device called the E-Meter, are designed to provide a path for individuals to achieve greater understanding and freedom. We'll explore these techniques and processes with examples and straightforward explanations to help you understand what auditing is, why it's so significant, and what it aims to accomplish.

In addition to these practices, we also go into Scientology's views on ethics, training, and communication. Scientologists value ethical behavior as a foundation for their beliefs, and they have a structured system to help individuals uphold these standards. Similarly, the importance of training and continuous learning is emphasized, with many courses designed to build both knowledge and self-awareness.

Finally, this book explores how Scientology views its place in the broader world. Scientology sees itself not only as a religion for individuals but also as a social movement with a role in contributing to the welfare of society. The last chapters touch on Scientology's vision for the future, its social programs, and its global outreach efforts.

We also look at popular questions among the public, such as why Scientology is so popular in Hollywood and perceived as so secretive.

We hope this book provides you with an insightful look into Scientology—its beliefs, practices, and aspirations. As you read, keep an open mind, and feel free to explore at your own pace. Scientology's language and approach to spirituality may be different from what you're used to, but each chapter is designed to guide you step by step, helping you make sense of this unique worldview.

Thank you for picking up this book, and may it answer your questions, spark new ideas, and broaden your perspective on the diverse paths people take in their search for understanding, purpose, and personal freedom.

# TOPICAL OUTLINE

**Chapter 1: Introduction to Scientology**
- The Origins of Scientology and L. Ron Hubbard
- The Purpose and Mission of Scientology
- Scientology's Influence and Global Reach
- Core Beliefs and Principles
- Key Terminology: Auditing, Thetan, and More
- The Structure and Organization of the Church of Scientology
- The Scientology Creed and Code of Honor
- Myths vs. Realities in Scientology
- Ethical Standards and Moral Codes
- The Journey of Self-Discovery in Scientology

**Chapter 2: The Concept of the Thetan**
- Understanding the Thetan as a Spiritual Being
- The Eternal Nature of the Thetan
- The Relationship Between Thetan, Mind, and Body
- The Role of the Thetan in Self-Improvement

**Chapter 3: The Dynamics of Existence**
- The First Dynamic: The Self
- The Second Dynamic: Family and Relationships
- The Third and Fourth Dynamics: Groups and Mankind
- The Eighth Dynamic and the Concept of Infinity
- Balancing All Eight Dynamics for Holistic Growth

**Chapter 4: The Mind and Scientology**
- The Analytical Mind vs. the Reactive Mind
- The Engram: Source of Mental and Emotional Pain
- Mechanisms of the Mind: How it Affects Actions and Choices
- The Importance of Mental Clarity in Scientology

**Chapter 5: The Bridge to Total Freedom**
- The Purpose of the Bridge
- Key Levels and Steps on the Bridge
- Moving from Pre-Clear to Clear Status
- Achieving Freedom from Limitations
- The Role of Personal Responsibility on the Bridge

**Chapter 6: Auditing – The Path to Self-Discovery**
- Definition and Purpose of Auditing
- The Role of the E-Meter in Auditing
- Processes and Techniques in Auditing

## Chapter 14: Scientology and Personal Development
- The Path to Self-Improvement and Realization
- Discovering Personal Potential and Strengths
- Overcoming Negative Influences and Behaviors
- Building Emotional Resilience
- Developing Discipline and Consistency in Practice

## Chapter 15: Scientology in Society
- Scientology's Social Programs and Initiatives
- Community Outreach and Social Justice
- Scientology's View on World Peace and Coexistence
- Why Is Scientology So Popular in Hollywood?
- Why Is Scientology Considered Secretive?
- Advocating for Human Rights and Equality

## Chapter 16: The Future of Scientology
- The Vision of a Clear Planet
- Growth and Expansion of Scientology
- Scientology's Role in Modern Spirituality and Society
- Adaptation to Technological and Cultural Changes

## Appendix
- Terms and Definitions

## Afterword

# TABLE OF CONTENTS

# CHAPTER 1: INTRODUCTION TO SCIENTOLOGY

## The Origins of Scientology and L. Ron Hubbard

L. Ron Hubbard founded Scientology in the early 1950s, a period marked by curiosity about psychology, spirituality, and human potential. Born on March 13, 1911, in Tilden, Nebraska, Hubbard showed early interests in science, literature, and adventure. His early life set the stage for the ideas he would later develop into a philosophy and eventually a worldwide religion. By combining his studies of Eastern and Western philosophies, his experiences as a writer, and his knowledge of psychology and science fiction, Hubbard crafted a distinctive worldview that would become the basis of Scientology.

**Hubbard's early experiences helped shape his unique approach**. His father, a U.S. naval officer, moved the family frequently, which exposed Hubbard to diverse cultures and perspectives. As a child and teenager, he lived in Guam and traveled throughout Asia, experiences that introduced him to Eastern philosophies, religions, and practices. Hubbard later described these formative travels as key to his understanding of the mind and spirit. He became fascinated by the human experience and what he perceived as universal spiritual truths, which he would later blend with Western scientific approaches. These experiences allowed him to study a variety of traditions, such as Buddhism and Taoism, that would later influence his spiritual philosophy.

After returning to the United States, Hubbard attended George Washington University in Washington, D.C., where he studied engineering. Although he left before completing his degree, he gained a scientific perspective that would influence his methods and theories. Engineering required analytical thinking, problem-solving, and an understanding of systems—all principles he would later apply to the workings of the mind and spirit. Hubbard's academic background contributed to his belief that a systematic, almost mechanical approach could help individuals resolve mental barriers and unlock their full potential. He described his future teachings not as mere beliefs but as "technologies" or "sciences" that could be applied and tested.

In the 1930s and 1940s, Hubbard became known as a prolific pulp fiction writer, particularly in the genres of science fiction and adventure. His stories often explored themes of exploration, survival, and the unknown, which allowed him to reach a wide audience and develop his writing skills. By the late 1930s, he had published numerous stories and even authored a bestselling novel, *Buckskin Brigades*. Although Hubbard's fiction and the world of Scientology might seem worlds apart, his experience as a writer shaped his ideas about human potential, survival, and the mind's influence on reality. This literary background later had a role in his ability to craft engaging, persuasive teachings and narratives within Scientology.

**Hubbard's approach to the mind took a significant step forward with the publication of *Dianetics: The Modern Science of Mental Health* in 1950.** Dianetics, which means "through the mind," was Hubbard's first attempt at presenting his theories on human consciousness, memory, and the mind's influence on physical and emotional health. In *Dianetics*, Hubbard introduced the concept of the "reactive mind," a part of the mind he described as storing painful memories, known as "engrams." According to Hubbard, engrams, often from traumatic events, could cause individuals to act irrationally and prevent them from reaching their full potential. By identifying and processing these engrams, he claimed that a person could free themselves from unwanted fears, negative emotions, and mental blocks. This process, called "auditing," would later become a core practice in Scientology.

*Dianetics* captured public interest, quickly becoming a bestseller and leading to the establishment of the first Dianetics centers across the United States. People from various backgrounds attended these centers, seeking personal transformation and a sense of empowerment through Hubbard's techniques. Although Dianetics initially focused on mental health, Hubbard eventually expanded his philosophy to address broader spiritual concepts. He began describing humans not just as minds and bodies but as "thetan," an immortal spiritual being that transcends the physical self. This idea of the thetan became a cornerstone of Scientology.

**In 1953, Hubbard formally established Scientology as a religion.** He argued that *Dianetics* dealt with the mind, while Scientology explored the spirit and the universe's ultimate questions. Hubbard maintained that Scientology offered a path to spiritual freedom, self-discovery, and heightened awareness of one's place in the universe. The religion promised that, by following specific teachings and practices, individuals could gain control over their lives, achieve clarity, and ultimately reach a state of total spiritual freedom. Unlike traditional Western religions, which often emphasize faith or divine intervention, Scientology's approach to spirituality focused on personal agency, self-discipline, and self-discovery. Hubbard believed that each person could gain spiritual enlightenment through systematic practices and teachings, rather than relying solely on faith.

Scientology grew rapidly as Hubbard continued to develop its doctrines and practices. He introduced a series of steps, known as "The Bridge to Total Freedom," which outlined the path for spiritual advancement within Scientology. This path included various levels of training and "processing," through which Scientologists could gradually increase their awareness and understanding of themselves as spiritual beings. Central to this journey was the process of auditing, a structured form of counseling intended to help individuals confront and release negative memories and emotions. Auditing became a defining feature of Scientology, as it promised to provide a tangible way to achieve personal breakthroughs.

Over the next two decades, Hubbard established numerous churches and centers globally, creating an extensive network of institutions to support Scientology's growth. He traveled, lectured, and authored an extensive collection of writings, many of which are now considered foundational Scientology texts. He also created various Scientology organizations, such as the Sea Organization, a group of dedicated Scientologists who help manage and oversee the church's activities worldwide. By the late 1960s and early 1970s, Hubbard's leadership extended across continents, and Scientology had become a complex, international organization with its own structure, beliefs, and practices.

Hubbard's teachings continually evolved, encompassing more than just spiritual principles. He developed courses on topics like communication, ethics, and personal development, each intended to provide Scientologists with practical skills to improve their lives. These courses emphasized personal responsibility, effective communication, and ethical behavior, values that Hubbard believed were essential for anyone pursuing spiritual growth. Through this focus on self-improvement and discipline, Hubbard positioned Scientology as a comprehensive way of life rather than a set of isolated beliefs.

Hubbard's influence on Scientology remains deeply ingrained, as nearly every practice, principle, and organizational structure traces back to his ideas. His writings, which encompass thousands of pages of text and numerous recorded lectures, are considered the central source of knowledge within Scientology. The church regards Hubbard as its "source," a term that reflects the view that his insights are not only foundational but essential to understanding the full scope of Scientology. Followers study his teachings extensively, believing that the knowledge he imparted is critical for achieving spiritual advancement.

While Hubbard passed away in 1986, Scientology continues to follow his principles, maintaining his writings and lectures as the definitive guide for all members. His legacy lives on through the religion's practices, its expansive organizational structure, and the dedicated followers who view his teachings as a pathway to spiritual clarity and empowerment. For Scientologists, L. Ron Hubbard's life represents a journey of discovery, resilience, and dedication to a vision that has now reached millions around the world. His contributions to Scientology remain central to its identity and purpose, shaping its future as it continues to expand and adapt.

## The Purpose and Mission of Scientology

Scientology defines its purpose as the spiritual betterment of the individual and humanity. Founded by L. Ron Hubbard, the church aims to provide tools for people to understand their spiritual essence, known as the "thetan." Hubbard believed that each person is a thetan—a spiritual being that is distinct from both mind and body. The mission of Scientology is to help individuals understand and fully realize their thetan nature, claiming that spiritual enlightenment brings self-awareness, mental clarity, and personal freedom. According to Scientology, discovering the true self allows individuals to live free from unwanted emotions and limitations.

Central to Scientology's mission is what it calls "The Bridge to Total Freedom," a systematic path that leads members to spiritual enlightenment and inner clarity. This Bridge represents levels of personal progress and is broken down into distinct steps, each designed to bring individuals closer to understanding themselves as spiritual beings. These levels are achieved through "processing" and "training," where processing focuses on self-exploration and resolving past traumas, while training teaches skills for personal development. Scientologists believe that moving up the Bridge allows them to handle life's challenges more effectively and ultimately reach a state called "Clear," where one is free from the influence of painful memories or "engrams."

Scientology's purpose extends beyond individual self-improvement, aiming to achieve what it calls "a world without insanity, without criminals, and without war." The church operates on the belief that, by improving individuals' lives, society as a whole will also transform. Scientologists view themselves as agents of change, working not only for personal growth but also to contribute positively to communities and the world. Through courses and outreach programs, Scientology seeks to instill ethical values, personal responsibility, and mental resilience, which it believes are essential for creating a peaceful and harmonious society.

The Church of Scientology operates various social programs as part of its mission to make the world a better place. These programs include drug rehabilitation, literacy campaigns, and prison reform, all designed to address what the church views as societal crises. One of the prominent efforts is Narconon, a drug rehabilitation program that claims to offer a path to sobriety through Scientology's methods. Through its social initiatives, Scientology aims to reach people who may not necessarily join the church but can benefit from its methods and philosophy.

**A core part of Scientology's purpose is education.** The church believes that ignorance and lack of awareness keep people from reaching their potential. To address this, Scientology provides numerous courses and training programs intended to improve communication, personal ethics, and interpersonal skills. By improving these areas, Scientologists believe individuals can better handle life's challenges and make more ethical decisions, contributing positively to society.

Scientology's mission is also about addressing what it perceives as barriers to personal and societal progress. Hubbard identified certain institutions, particularly psychiatry, as opposing forces to spiritual well-being. Scientology maintains that psychiatry and psychotropic drugs can suppress human potential by focusing only on the physical aspects of mental health, ignoring the spiritual dimension. Through its Citizens Commission on Human Rights (CCHR), Scientology campaigns against psychiatric practices it considers abusive, advocating for spiritual rather than chemical approaches to mental health. In this way, Scientology positions itself as a movement aimed at "saving humanity" from practices it sees as harmful.

The church encourages its members to share their faith actively, with the goal of reaching as many people as possible. Scientologists believe that helping others discover their spiritual nature is a fundamental responsibility. The church's mission to spread its teachings is often carried out through local Scientology centers and public events. Books, lectures, and online materials are used to introduce newcomers to Scientology, aiming to reach those who might benefit from its philosophy of self-empowerment. Through these efforts, the church promotes the view that Scientology offers a path to greater understanding, self-mastery, and peace.

The church's structured approach to achieving its mission is unique, as it seeks to systematize spiritual enlightenment and personal improvement. Unlike some spiritual paths that focus on individual journeys without set steps, Scientology's Bridge to Total Freedom provides a specific and organized route to what it considers enlightenment. This structure appeals to individuals who desire a clear, defined path for growth. Scientology's courses and auditing sessions are designed to be consistent, with methods and processes that followers believe yield predictable results. This predictability is presented as a key advantage of Scientology's approach to spirituality and personal development.

Scientology's mission also encompasses what it calls "Clearing the Planet." This phrase signifies the goal of creating a world where every person has reached a state of mental clarity and spiritual awareness. The church believes that a world with "Clears" will be more ethical, harmonious, and free from conflict. For Scientologists, this ultimate goal is worth working toward on both personal and societal levels. The church considers each individual who progresses on the Bridge a step closer to making this vision a reality.

Scientology's purpose and mission, therefore, are twofold: the personal transformation of its members and the broader transformation of society. The church operates on the belief that these two goals are interconnected. Personal growth, according to Scientology, enables individuals to make positive contributions to the world. Through its teachings, outreach, and global mission, Scientology seeks to create an environment where every person can discover their potential and live in harmony with others.

## Scientology's Influence and Global Reach

Since its establishment in the 1950s, Scientology has expanded from a small movement into a global organization. The church claims to have millions of members across numerous countries, with centers in cities around the world. Its global reach is supported by extensive infrastructure, including churches, missions, and social programs. Headquartered in Los Angeles, California, Scientology maintains a network of churches across continents, including major centers in the United Kingdom, Australia, South Africa, and across Europe. This international presence helps Scientology spread its teachings and expand its influence to diverse communities.

Scientology's growth is partly due to its ability to establish itself in various cultural contexts. Scientology aims to provide a universal approach to spiritual growth, one that does not depend on nationality, ethnicity, or previous religious beliefs. Its teachings are presented as applicable to all people, regardless of background. This universality is central to Scientology's appeal in diverse cultural settings. The church often emphasizes that it welcomes individuals from any faith, although it ultimately encourages members to prioritize Scientology teachings as their primary spiritual path.

The church uses various media channels to promote its philosophy and attract new followers. Scientology has invested in television, radio, print, and digital platforms to spread its message. In 2018, the church launched the Scientology Network, a 24-hour TV channel that provides programming on its beliefs, practices, and community initiatives. The network aims to demystify Scientology, offering an insider's view of its global activities and success stories from members. This media presence allows Scientology to reach a wider audience, aiming to clarify its purpose and counter criticisms or misconceptions.

A significant part of Scientology's global influence comes from its social programs, which operate under the banner of humanitarian work. These programs, like Narconon (drug rehabilitation), Applied Scholastics (education), and The Way to Happiness (moral values), are often presented as secular initiatives. While they promote Scientology's philosophy, these programs aim to attract a broad audience, including people who may not be interested in joining the church but are receptive to its self-help methods. Through these programs, Scientology extends its impact beyond religious members, reaching individuals in crisis situations or seeking personal improvement.

Scientology's *Freewinds* ship, which functions as a training center and symbol of international outreach, serves as another way the church expands its influence. The *Freewinds* hosts high-level courses, events, and retreats for Scientologists, and its itinerant nature allows the church to connect with different countries and communities. By holding international conventions and events on the ship, Scientology strengthens its global network and unites members from various regions.

The church's emphasis on self-improvement and structured growth has also helped it gain traction among individuals seeking practical skills and personal advancement. Courses on communication, ethics, and problem-solving are popular within Scientology, and these are designed to offer value beyond religious or spiritual aspects. Scientologists often describe their courses as tools for achieving greater success in life, whether in relationships, career, or personal well-being. This focus on practical skills and structured progress attracts people from many walks of life.

Despite criticism from some quarters, Scientology remains active in promoting its beliefs and mission worldwide. The church uses its global reach to counter negative portrayals and present its version of events. Scientology's PR strategies, community events, and high-profile members, including prominent actors, all contribute to a positive image, especially in countries where its presence is well-established.

Through consistent outreach, international media, and a vast network of facilities, Scientology continues to expand its reach, promoting what it believes to be a universal message of spiritual freedom and personal empowerment.

## Core Beliefs and Principles

Scientology's beliefs and principles revolve around the idea that humans are spiritual beings with untapped potential. Scientologists believe that each person is a **"thetan"**, an immortal spirit that transcends physical form, thought to be inherently good, capable, and divine in origin. This thetan is separate from the mind and body, with its own thoughts, awareness, and perspective. Unlike many religious views, Scientology asserts that a person's true self is not bound by their physical body or mind; rather, the thetan uses the mind and body as instruments to interact with the physical world.

At the heart of Scientology's approach is a strong focus on **self-awareness and self-empowerment**. Scientologists believe that every individual has inherent knowledge and power that can be realized through a process of spiritual development and self-discovery. This journey, often described as the "Bridge to Total Freedom," is structured as a step-by-step path designed to help the individual understand and strengthen their spiritual identity. This Bridge consists of a series of specific levels and practices that one must complete to move closer to enlightenment. Each level represents a new stage of spiritual awareness and progress, leading ultimately to greater understanding and self-empowerment.

Central to Scientology's worldview is the belief that the mind is divided into two parts: the **analytical mind** and the **reactive mind**. The analytical mind is considered the rational part, functioning logically and able to make clear decisions. It operates like a computer, analyzing data and solving problems based on facts and experience. The reactive mind, however, is where Scientology places the root of all negative thoughts, emotions, and destructive behaviors. This part of the mind is associated with engrams, which are painful memories from traumatic events. Scientologists believe that these engrams are stored in the reactive mind and are activated during moments of stress, causing irrational or self-destructive behavior. The process of "clearing" the reactive mind of engrams is fundamental to Scientology's approach to mental health and personal freedom.

A key goal of Scientology is to reach a state known as **"Clear."** A Clear, according to Scientology, is someone who has successfully erased all engrams from their reactive mind. Being Clear is considered a transformative achievement, marking the beginning of an individual's true spiritual journey. Once an individual reaches Clear, they are believed to gain control over their thoughts, emotions, and reactions, free from the influence of painful memories. Clear individuals are thought to experience improved mental clarity, higher intelligence, and better emotional well-being. This state is seen as a necessary step on the path toward achieving full spiritual enlightenment.

Beyond Clear, Scientology offers a series of advanced spiritual states known as the **Operating Thetan (OT) levels**. These levels aim to increase a person's spiritual abilities, granting them greater understanding and control over themselves and their environment. OT levels are intended for those who have already reached Clear and are ready for more profound spiritual exploration. Operating Thetans are believed to be individuals who have realized their full spiritual potential, possessing abilities beyond those of average individuals, including heightened perceptions and insights. The final OT level, OT VIII, is the highest level currently available, and reaching this stage is seen as a significant achievement within Scientology.

**The Eight Dynamics** are another core concept within Scientology, representing various areas of life and existence through which individuals express themselves. The first four dynamics cover personal and social relationships: the First Dynamic is the self; the Second Dynamic is family and procreation; the Third Dynamic is groups and organizations; and the Fourth Dynamic is humanity as a whole. The higher dynamics extend beyond human relationships: the Fifth Dynamic encompasses all living things, the Sixth Dynamic includes the physical universe, the Seventh Dynamic represents spirituality, and the Eighth Dynamic refers to the Supreme Being or infinity. Scientologists believe that understanding and balancing these eight dynamics helps individuals live harmoniously with themselves and others.

In addition to individual development, Scientology also emphasizes the importance of **ethics** and **personal integrity**. Ethics in Scientology are not just rules but principles that guide behavior in alignment with what is considered "survival" for oneself and the group. Scientologists are encouraged to live ethically to ensure they contribute positively to the community and their own lives. Personal integrity is viewed as a core value, meaning that each individual should act in accordance with their inner beliefs and values rather than societal expectations or pressures. Scientology's ethics system includes various procedures to address ethical lapses and restore integrity, providing a structured approach to resolving conflicts and upholding personal responsibility.

Another critical element of Scientology is **communication**. Hubbard developed a series of communication exercises known as "Training Routines" (TRs), which are designed to improve an individual's communication skills. These exercises are meant to increase one's ability to understand and interact with others, as well as to maintain focus and remain calm under pressure. Scientologists believe that effective communication is essential for spiritual growth and social harmony, as it enables individuals to express themselves clearly and resolve misunderstandings.

The **Scientology Creed** outlines the church's beliefs about human rights and dignity. It asserts that all individuals have the right to think freely, speak freely, and choose their own beliefs. This creed reflects Scientology's emphasis on individual freedom and personal autonomy, values that are central to its mission. Additionally, the creed affirms that all individuals are spiritual beings deserving of respect and the right to pursue their own understanding of life and existence.

Scientology teaches that individuals can achieve happiness and success through a process called **"applied knowledge."** This principle holds that understanding and applying knowledge to real-life situations is key to achieving personal and spiritual goals. Scientologists believe that knowledge is only valuable when it is actively used, and they are encouraged to apply the teachings of Scientology to their daily lives. This practical application is seen as essential for personal growth and is encouraged throughout all levels of Scientology's training and processing.

Lastly, **Scientology views its role as contributing to global betterment** through social initiatives. Scientologists are encouraged to engage in activities that promote literacy, drug rehabilitation, human rights, and social justice. Programs such as Narconon (drug rehabilitation), Criminon (criminal reform), and Applied Scholastics (education) are designed to improve society by addressing specific issues and providing practical solutions rooted in Hubbard's teachings. Through these initiatives, Scientology seeks to create a world where people can live ethically and reach their full potential, aligning with its broader goal of "Clearing the Planet."

## Key Terminology: Auditing, Thetan, and More

Auditing, thetan, and other unique terms are central to understanding Scientology. **Auditing** is a core practice in Scientology, where individuals work one-on-one with an auditor to confront and address painful memories or traumas, called "engrams." Using a device called the E-Meter, auditors help individuals identify these engrams and release negative emotions tied to them, aiming to achieve mental clarity and progress toward the state of "Clear."

A **thetan** is the spiritual essence of each person, considered the true self beyond the mind and body. Scientologists believe the thetan is immortal and exists independent of the physical world, capable of self-realization and spiritual growth.

In addition to auditing and thetan, Scientology has many other terms and concepts, such as "Operating Thetan" (OT), "reactive mind," and "engrams." Each has a specific role within the teachings and practices of Scientology, contributing to its structured approach to personal and spiritual development.

For a complete list of Scientology's terminology, refer to the **Appendix** at the end of this book, which provides definitions and explanations for these and other important terms.

# The Structure and Organization of the Church of Scientology

The Church of Scientology is organized in a hierarchical structure, with a clear system for managing its activities and overseeing the spiritual progress of its members. At its core, the Church aims to deliver Scientology's teachings, guide individuals on their spiritual paths, and maintain its international presence. The main organizational hub is known as the **Church of Scientology International (CSI)**, headquartered in Los Angeles, California. This central body coordinates global activities, ensures the consistency of Scientology practices, and sets guidelines for all local churches, missions, and affiliated organizations.

One of the most prominent divisions within the Church is the **Sea Organization**, or Sea Org, established by L. Ron Hubbard in 1967. Originally conceived as a naval-based group that operated aboard ships, the Sea Org now operates as the most dedicated and senior-level organization within the Church. Sea Org members are considered the "elite" of Scientology, with each member pledging a symbolic "billion-year contract" to signify their lifelong commitment to the Church. Members of the Sea Org are responsible for managing the Church's key operations, including the training and auditing of advanced levels. They oversee regional and global centers and often hold influential roles within the Church's international management.

At the regional level, **continental organizations** oversee Scientology's presence across specific areas such as Europe, Latin America, Asia, and Africa. These continental centers provide support to local churches, ensure uniform practices, and manage the distribution of Scientology materials. Continental organizations are overseen by the Sea Org and CSI to maintain alignment with the Church's mission and objectives. In addition to managing these centers, continental organizations conduct special events, conferences, and seminars to encourage members' spiritual growth and promote Church initiatives.

Local Scientology churches, also known as **"orgs"** (short for "organizations"), operate in cities around the world and serve as the primary places where Scientology's teachings are delivered to the public. These local churches provide introductory courses, auditing sessions, and counseling for new and existing members. They are structured to deliver the initial stages of "The Bridge to Total Freedom," and local orgs act as community centers, hosting events, study groups, and public outreach efforts. Each local church is led by an executive director who manages staff, coordinates activities, and ensures that the Church's practices are followed accurately. This consistency is reinforced by the CSI and continental organizations, which oversee the training of staff at local churches.

Scientology also has **missions**, which are smaller, community-based centers that provide an introduction to Scientology in regions where the Church is less established. Missions offer basic auditing, introductory courses, and information sessions, but they typically do not deliver the more advanced levels available in larger orgs. Often staffed by volunteers, missions serve as an outreach tool for Scientology, allowing newcomers to engage with the religion in a more accessible, localized setting. Missions can eventually grow into full orgs if membership and resources increase, which is part of Scientology's expansion strategy.

Education is central to the Church's structure, with many members advancing through **Scientology's training centers**. These centers focus on auditor training, allowing members to learn the skills required to conduct auditing sessions. Scientologists believe that trained auditors are essential to achieving spiritual progress, and the training programs ensure that the Church has a reliable pool of auditors worldwide. Auditor training occurs at every level of the Church, from local orgs to advanced centers, where members can pursue training for higher levels on the Bridge to Total Freedom.

Advanced training and higher-level auditing are conducted at **Flag Service Organization (FSO)** in Clearwater, Florida, known as "Flag." This location is regarded as one of the most significant centers in Scientology, often considered the "spiritual headquarters" of the Church. Flag offers advanced auditing services and specialized training that are not available in other orgs, making it a destination for Scientologists seeking to complete higher OT (Operating Thetan) levels. Flag is operated by Sea Org members, and it is viewed as a place of pilgrimage within the Church, where members from around the world come to progress in their spiritual journey.

The **Freewinds**, a Scientology ship based in the Caribbean, serves a unique role as a training center for the highest levels of OT. The Freewinds is the only place where members can complete OT VIII, the highest current level of spiritual progression in Scientology. The ship is also used for conventions, retreats, and spiritual events, providing a secluded environment for advanced training. The Freewinds is managed by the Sea Org, and its exclusivity makes it an esteemed location within the Church, symbolizing a commitment to spiritual advancement and the achievement of ultimate spiritual clarity.

Scientology's structure also includes **social programs and outreach initiatives** that operate under separate organizations affiliated with the Church. Programs like Narconon (for drug rehabilitation), Criminon (for criminal rehabilitation), and Applied Scholastics (for education) are designed to address societal issues, often in collaboration with communities outside of Scientology. Although these programs are based on Hubbard's teachings, they are presented as secular initiatives, and they reach people who may not be interested in joining the Church itself. These programs extend Scientology's influence beyond its membership, promoting its values and principles to the wider public.

In addition to its hierarchy of training and operational centers, the Church has various **management bodies** responsible for legal and administrative functions. The Religious Technology Center (RTC) holds the trademarks and copyrights related to Scientology, ensuring that Hubbard's works are preserved and that Church practices remain true to his original teachings. RTC's role includes protecting the intellectual property of Scientology and overseeing the use of its symbols, texts, and materials across all affiliated organizations. RTC reports directly to CSI, creating a system of checks and balances within the Church's organizational framework.

The Church of Scientology's structure reflects its goal of providing a clear path for spiritual advancement and ensuring the consistency of its practices worldwide. This well-defined hierarchy allows for a coordinated approach to outreach, training, and community service, with each level of the Church supporting its members' journey on the Bridge to Total Freedom.

## The Scientology Creed and Code of Honor

The **Scientology Creed** outlines the core beliefs of Scientology, addressing the inherent rights and dignity of all individuals. Written by L. Ron Hubbard in 1954, the Creed serves as a declaration of values that emphasizes the spiritual equality of all people. It states that everyone has an inalienable right to think freely, speak freely, and live according to their beliefs, regardless of race, nationality, or faith. The Creed asserts that humans are fundamentally good and capable, with the potential to achieve spiritual enlightenment. For Scientologists, this statement of beliefs defines their commitment to personal growth and the belief that all individuals have a right to pursue their understanding of life and spirituality.

One of the Creed's central principles is the **recognition of human rights**, which Hubbard described as essential for a peaceful and just society. The Creed includes a commitment to freedom of expression and belief, stating that everyone has the right to their own opinions and that no one should be persecuted for their beliefs. This principle reflects Scientology's opposition to what it considers oppressive systems, including practices that attempt to suppress or control individual thought. Scientologists see the Creed as affirming their dedication to a world where all people can explore and express their spiritual selves without interference.

Another key aspect of the Creed is the belief that people have the **right to self-determination and personal responsibility**. According to the Creed, each individual is responsible for their actions and has the right to choose their own path. Scientologists interpret this as a call to live ethically and take responsibility for one's actions, decisions, and their impact on others. The Creed emphasizes that, by choosing personal accountability and ethical conduct, individuals can achieve spiritual growth and positively contribute to society.

The **Code of Honor** is a complementary set of guidelines that Scientologists are encouraged to follow in their daily lives. While the Creed is a statement of universal values, the Code of Honor serves as a more personal ethical standard for Scientologists, outlining specific behaviors that reflect integrity, loyalty, and self-respect. It includes principles like "never compromise with your own reality" and "be true to your own goals." These statements are intended to guide Scientologists in maintaining authenticity and self-respect, promoting a lifestyle aligned with their spiritual beliefs.

The Code of Honor also emphasizes **loyalty to one's group and to humanity as a whole**. Scientologists are encouraged to support each other and work toward collective goals, viewing the Code as a way to build unity and foster a positive community. This loyalty is considered crucial in achieving Scientology's broader mission, as it encourages members to support each other's growth and promote a supportive environment for personal and spiritual advancement. Scientologists believe that by following the Code, they strengthen their commitment to both their own development and the betterment of society.

The **Code of Honor includes directives against abandoning personal principles**, even under external pressure. Scientologists are encouraged to "never desert a group to which you owe your support," and to "never permit your affinity to be alloyed." These guidelines are viewed as a way to maintain personal integrity, allowing members to remain consistent with their values. By adhering to the Code of Honor, Scientologists aim to create a foundation of trust and reliability within their community, believing that integrity leads to greater spiritual clarity.

Both the Creed and Code of Honor serve as a moral compass for Scientologists, guiding their actions and interactions with others. These texts encourage Scientologists to live with integrity, pursue spiritual freedom, and respect the rights of others. Scientologists see these documents as essential tools for personal growth, helping them navigate life with principles that support their journey on the Bridge to Total Freedom.

# Myths vs. Realities in Scientology

Scientology, as a relatively modern religion, has attracted significant public attention and, along with it, numerous myths and misconceptions. These misunderstandings can arise from the church's unique terminology, practices, and secretive aspects of its advanced teachings. Here, we'll separate some of the most common myths from the realities in Scientology, providing a clearer understanding of what the church truly teaches, believes, and practices.

### Myth 1: Scientology is Anti-Science
A common misconception is that Scientology rejects science and scientific principles. In reality, Scientology does not dismiss science; rather, it seeks to integrate elements of scientific approaches into spiritual practices. Founder L. Ron Hubbard himself studied engineering and applied a methodical approach to his theories on the mind, mental health, and personal development. Scientology claims to be rooted in "scientific" principles, referring to its practices as "applied religious philosophy." However, critics argue that Scientology's practices and claims,

particularly those surrounding the E-Meter and auditing, are not scientifically validated. Scientologists, meanwhile, maintain that the church's techniques are meant to enhance one's spiritual understanding and are not necessarily "scientific" in the traditional sense.

## Myth 2: Scientology is a "Cult" Focused on Mind Control

The label of "cult" is often used to describe Scientology, with claims that the church uses manipulative tactics to control its members. While it's true that Scientology has a strict organizational structure and certain behaviors and practices are encouraged, Scientologists counter that the church respects individual freedom and autonomy. Members choose to participate in the church's services, and auditing, for example, is a voluntary practice. The intense commitment seen in some Scientologists can resemble devotion in other religions. Critics often misunderstand the church's structured hierarchy and extensive system of courses as controlling, while members argue that these are tools for spiritual advancement. They assert that Scientology encourages personal responsibility and self-discovery rather than dependence on the church.

## Myth 3: The E-Meter is a "Lie Detector"

One persistent myth is that the E-Meter, an instrument used in auditing, functions as a lie detector. The E-Meter measures electrical resistance on the skin through a small, harmless current, which Scientologists believe indicates areas of emotional or mental significance during auditing. Contrary to popular belief, the E-Meter doesn't detect lies or provide any definitive "truth." Instead, it's used as a tool to help individuals uncover thoughts and memories that may be influencing their mental state. Critics often question the effectiveness and validity of the E-Meter, as it lacks scientific validation outside of Scientology. Scientologists, however, maintain that it is an essential part of auditing, helping them identify and address hidden issues within the reactive mind.

## Myth 4: Scientology is Only for the Wealthy

Another myth is that Scientology is exclusively for the wealthy, as its courses, auditing sessions, and advanced services are known to be costly. While it's true that Scientology services often come with fees, the church argues that its teachings are available to anyone who sincerely wants to learn, regardless of financial status. Scientology organizations offer free introductory materials, such as pamphlets, books, and videos, to those interested in learning about the basics of the faith. Critics, however, contend that many of Scientology's advanced teachings are financially out of reach for lower-income individuals, which can create an impression that it's a religion for the elite. Scientologists counter this claim by pointing to various payment options, scholarships, and volunteer-based exchange programs that can help make participation more accessible.

## Myth 5: Scientologists Worship L. Ron Hubbard

There is a belief that Scientologists revere L. Ron Hubbard as a divine or god-like figure, similar to the founders of other religions. In reality, Scientologists do not worship Hubbard but regard him as an influential thinker, teacher, and "Source" of their spiritual knowledge. Hubbard is respected for his contributions, teachings, and discoveries, and his works are studied extensively within the church. His image is commonly displayed in Scientology centers, and his birthday is celebrated, but the church emphasizes that this respect does not equate to worship. Scientologists see Hubbard as a guide and an architect of the church, not as a divine figure.

## Myth 6: Scientology is Anti-Psychiatry Because It Denies Mental Illness

A frequently held misconception is that Scientology denies the existence of mental illness because of its strong opposition to psychiatry. While Scientology does critique psychiatric practices, particularly the use of psychotropic drugs, it does not claim that mental distress or emotional issues are nonexistent. Instead, Scientology promotes a spiritual approach to addressing mental health challenges, focusing on auditing and self-improvement rather than medication. Through practices like auditing, Scientologists aim to confront and handle negative emotions and past traumas. The church argues that psychiatric drugs treat symptoms rather than underlying causes, which Scientology addresses spiritually. Critics argue that this stance can discourage members from seeking conventional mental health care, but Scientologists view their approach as an alternative rather than a denial of mental suffering.

## Myth 7: Scientology Is Secretive About Its Beliefs

Scientology's secrecy, particularly about its advanced teachings, has led to the perception that it has hidden or even sinister doctrines. Some beliefs and teachings are indeed only accessible to members who have reached certain levels of spiritual advancement, such as the Operating Thetan (OT) levels. The Church of Scientology explains that these teachings are reserved for advanced practitioners because they require a foundational understanding of earlier levels. While this practice is similar to initiatory secrets in other religions and fraternities, critics view it as an attempt to conceal controversial or unusual beliefs. Scientologists argue that these advanced teachings are simply part of a structured path and are only fully meaningful to those who have completed the earlier stages.

## Myth 8: Scientology Claims to be the Only Path to Salvation

Some believe that Scientology presents itself as the exclusive route to salvation, dismissing other religions. In reality, Scientology describes itself as compatible with other faiths, emphasizing personal experience and spiritual growth over dogma. Scientology teaches that individuals can explore their spirituality in various ways and do not have to abandon their existing beliefs to study Scientology. However, the church does encourage members to dedicate themselves fully to Scientology's teachings as they advance, often leading individuals to adopt Scientology as their primary belief system. Scientologists believe their path offers a unique understanding of the spirit but recognize that each person's journey is their own.

## Myth 9: Scientology Does Not Believe in God or a Supreme Being

A common myth is that Scientology lacks a belief in a higher power or God. While Scientology does not have a specific concept of God, as seen in many traditional religions, it acknowledges a higher reality, which it calls the "Eighth Dynamic" or "Infinity." Scientology leaves the interpretation of this concept open to individual understanding, allowing members to form their views on the existence and nature of a Supreme Being. Rather than dictating a concrete definition of God, Scientology emphasizes personal spiritual discovery and the thetan's relationship with the universe. For Scientologists, the focus is on their personal spiritual journey rather than a defined notion of God.

**Myth 10: Scientology is Anti-Family**
A persistent myth is that Scientology discourages family bonds and relationships outside the church. However, Scientology actually places importance on family and the "Second Dynamic," which involves family, children, and relationships. Scientologists believe that strengthening family connections is part of an ethical, fulfilling life. Nonetheless, some families have reported estrangement issues due to a practice called "disconnection," where members are advised to cut ties with individuals seen as a negative influence. Scientology presents disconnection as a way to protect personal well-being rather than as a policy against family, but critics argue it can lead to family separations. Scientologists maintain that family is valued and supported in the church as long as members are in alignment with Scientology's values.

**Myth 11: Scientology is Entirely Closed to Criticism**
Many believe that Scientology does not tolerate criticism or dissent, given its reputation for taking legal action against detractors. While the church does actively defend its teachings and image, Scientologists are encouraged to explore their beliefs and question their understanding. The church asserts that its methods are tested and repeatable, offering what it calls "exact knowledge." It also operates an ethics system that addresses criticism from within the church, guiding members to resolve conflicts while upholding Scientology's values. Members argue that discussions and disagreements are not discouraged but handled within a framework that protects the church's stability and mission.

Scientology's complexity and unconventional practices have made it the subject of both interest and scrutiny. Understanding these myths and their realities provides a more nuanced view of the church and its beliefs, helping clarify the values, teachings, and structure of Scientology for those who seek to learn more.


# Ethical Standards and Moral Codes


Scientology's ethical standards and moral codes are foundational to its teachings, guiding members in their interactions with others and in personal conduct. Unlike some religious ethics that rely on commandments or strict rules, Scientology's ethics are based on principles of personal responsibility and the promotion of survival. Scientology emphasizes that ethical behavior is not about blindly following rules; instead, it's about making decisions that enhance one's own well-being and contribute positively to society.

**Ethics in Scientology revolve around the concept of survival**, both for the individual and the broader community. Scientologists are taught to evaluate their actions by considering how they affect each of the Eight Dynamics—self, family, groups, humanity, life forms, the physical universe, spirituality, and infinity. A "good" action is one that supports the survival and flourishing of these dynamics, while a "bad" action is one that harms them. This framework encourages Scientologists to weigh their choices carefully and align their actions with the betterment of themselves and others.

Central to Scientology's ethical code is the **idea of personal responsibility**. Scientologists believe that each individual is accountable for their actions and that ethical behavior stems from this accountability. The Church teaches that understanding and embracing one's responsibility in life is essential to spiritual growth and self-improvement. As individuals advance in Scientology, they are encouraged to take increasing responsibility not only for themselves but also for their families, communities, and ultimately, the world.

Scientology's ethical system includes a structured approach to addressing ethical lapses, referred to as "ethics conditions." Members are encouraged to identify and rectify any actions that may have been harmful to themselves or others. This system has distinct levels, ranging from "non-existence" to "power," with specific guidelines for improving one's ethical standing. If a member is seen to be acting contrary to Scientology's values, they may undergo a process to restore their ethical condition, which could involve taking responsibility for past actions and demonstrating a commitment to ethical improvement.

In addition to personal responsibility, **the concept of integrity is highly emphasized** in Scientology's ethical framework. Integrity, in this context, means staying true to one's own beliefs and values, even when faced with external pressure. The Church encourages members to make decisions based on their understanding of what is right, rather than simply following societal norms or expectations. By maintaining personal integrity, Scientologists believe they can achieve a higher level of self-respect and spiritual clarity.

A complementary set of principles, called the **Code of Honor**, serves as a personal moral compass for Scientologists. This code outlines behaviors that reflect integrity, loyalty, and respect for oneself and others. It includes statements like "Never compromise with your own reality" and "Be true to your own goals," which remind members to stay aligned with their values and pursue personal and spiritual growth. The Code of Honor is not enforced but is seen as an aspirational guide, encouraging members to live authentically and responsibly.

Scientology also promotes a moral code known as **The Way to Happiness**, a booklet written by L. Ron Hubbard that contains 21 precepts for ethical living. These precepts cover areas such as honesty, respect for others, self-discipline, and responsibility toward family and society. Although not religious in nature, The Way to Happiness is intended to provide practical guidance for everyday life.

Scientologists distribute it widely as a public service, believing it can improve society by promoting ethical conduct.

Together, Scientology's ethical standards and moral codes provide a framework for decision-making and personal development. By focusing on personal responsibility, integrity, and respect for the Eight Dynamics, Scientologists aim to live in a way that supports their spiritual journey and contributes positively to society. These ethical principles are seen not only as pathways to individual happiness but as essential for creating a peaceful, cooperative, and thriving world.

## The Journey of Self-Discovery in Scientology

The journey of self-discovery in Scientology is a structured, progressive path toward understanding and realizing one's full potential as a spiritual being. Scientology teaches that each individual is more than just a body or a mind; they are a thetan, an immortal spirit with abilities, wisdom, and awareness that often lie dormant or undiscovered. This journey is mapped out through a series of steps known as **The Bridge to Total Freedom**, a guide to spiritual advancement designed to help individuals confront their past experiences, gain self-knowledge, and ultimately achieve a state of spiritual clarity and freedom.

The Bridge to Total Freedom consists of two main components: **processing** (often called auditing) and **training**. Processing involves one-on-one counseling sessions where the individual, or "preclear," works with an auditor to identify and release negative influences from the mind, particularly those stored in the reactive mind as "engrams." Engrams, according to Scientology, are harmful memories of past traumas that prevent individuals from achieving true happiness and self-awareness. By addressing these engrams in auditing sessions, the individual begins to free themselves from past limitations, gaining mental clarity and emotional stability.

As individuals progress through auditing, they work toward a state called **Clear**. Achieving Clear is seen as a significant milestone in Scientology, marking the point at which a person is no longer controlled by their reactive mind. In this state, the individual is believed to be free from irrational fears, unwanted emotions, and self-doubt, having resolved many of the negative influences that once held them back. Becoming Clear is viewed as an essential step in self-discovery, as it allows individuals to experience their true self without interference from past traumas. The journey does not end at Clear; it is simply the foundation for further spiritual exploration.

Once an individual reaches Clear, they can pursue **Operating Thetan (OT) levels**, a series of advanced spiritual levels aimed at enhancing the individual's awareness and control over their spiritual self. The OT levels are described as steps that help Scientologists achieve deeper insights, greater self-mastery, and an increased understanding of their role as spiritual beings. Each OT level is designed to address different aspects of spiritual awareness, guiding individuals to confront challenges and gain new abilities. Reaching higher OT levels is a gradual process, with each step offering new revelations and experiences that bring the Scientologist closer to a state of full spiritual freedom.

In addition to auditing, **training is important** in the journey of self-discovery. Scientology provides numerous courses that teach individuals how to enhance their communication skills, improve personal relationships, and increase their understanding of themselves and others. These courses, often referred to as "Training Routines" (TRs), involve practical exercises designed to help individuals remain focused, communicate effectively, and handle challenging situations. Training is seen as complementary to auditing, as it provides tools for day-to-day life, strengthening a person's ability to apply Scientology principles in real-world settings.

Throughout this journey, **the concept of personal responsibility** is consistently reinforced. Scientologists believe that true self-discovery requires an acceptance of one's responsibility for their actions, thoughts, and choices. This responsibility is not only personal but extends to one's family, community, and the world at large. Taking responsibility, according to Scientology, is an essential part of spiritual growth, as it empowers individuals to shape their lives and overcome obstacles. Through auditing and training, Scientologists aim to understand and manage their influence on others, promoting positive, ethical behavior as a result of self-awareness.

The journey of self-discovery in Scientology also emphasizes **integrity and ethical living**. Scientologists are encouraged to act in accordance with their beliefs and values, staying true to their personal goals and aspirations. Maintaining integrity is seen as essential for spiritual progress, as it allows individuals to live authentically, free from guilt or regret. By aligning their actions with the ethical standards of Scientology, individuals strive to live a life that supports both their personal goals and the well-being of those around them.

A unique aspect of self-discovery in Scientology is the **focus on the Eight Dynamics**, a framework that encourages Scientologists to view their lives in relation to various areas of existence. The first four dynamics cover the self, family, groups, and humanity, while the higher dynamics extend to all living things, the physical universe, spirituality, and infinity. By understanding these dynamics, individuals learn to consider how their actions affect different aspects of their lives, ultimately leading to a more harmonious and balanced existence. Each dynamic represents an area where Scientologists can explore their impact, making the Eight Dynamics an essential guide for self-discovery.

The journey of self-discovery in Scientology is continuous, with new challenges and revelations at each level. Rather than a single destination, Scientologists view self-discovery as an ongoing process of learning, growth, and improvement. As they progress along the Bridge to Total Freedom, they are encouraged to examine their beliefs, confront personal obstacles, and redefine their sense of self. This journey is deeply personal, with each individual experiencing their own path and pace, leading them closer to what Scientology describes as total spiritual freedom and enlightenment.

Through auditing, training, ethical responsibility, and a commitment to personal growth, Scientologists pursue a path they believe will lead them to a higher state of understanding, peace, and self-realization. For Scientologists, this journey of self-discovery is more than a series of teachings—it is a transformative path to understanding their true nature and purpose as spiritual beings.

# CHAPTER 2: THE CONCEPT OF THE THETAN

## Understanding the Thetan as a Spiritual Being

In Scientology, the concept of the thetan lies at the core of understanding human identity and existence. The thetan, as defined by L. Ron Hubbard, is the individual's true self—a spiritual being that exists independently of the body and mind. According to Scientology, this is not merely a soul or a vague essence but the actual source of consciousness, identity, and awareness within each person. The thetan is considered immortal, having existed before the body and mind and continuing to exist long after they're gone.

Hubbard described the thetan as *"you"*, not something you have but what you fundamentally are. Scientologists believe that the thetan has abilities, knowledge, and awareness that extend far beyond the physical world. It is capable of thought, creativity, and decision-making, and it is the part of you that experiences emotions, perceptions, and awareness. However, it can be constrained by physical and mental influences, which Scientology aims to address through its practices.

In Hubbard's teachings, **the thetan is ageless and has lived countless lives** across time and space. Scientologists consider the thetan to be both timeless and boundless, capable of occupying or discarding bodies as needed. This perspective on the thetan forms the basis for the belief in reincarnation, or what Scientologists often refer to as "past lives." Hubbard suggested that a thetan has accumulated experiences over millions of lifetimes, which impact their current life, often in ways they might not consciously understand. Scientology aims to uncover these influences, helping the thetan reach greater awareness and spiritual freedom.

The distinction between the thetan and the physical body is essential. The thetan, in Scientology's view, is not confined by physical limitations. While the body allows the thetan to interact with the material world, it is ultimately just a tool or vessel. This separation means that the thetan exists independently of physical states, such as health, age, or even death. Scientologists believe that through spiritual practices like auditing, they can gain a clearer perception of their identity as thetans, unbinding themselves from purely physical concerns.

Scientology teaches that the thetan has been subject to various influences and restrictions over time, leading to what is called the "reactive mind." This reactive mind, filled with painful memories and traumas, often obscures the thetan's true nature. In its pure state, the thetan is seen as highly capable and free from the negative influences that accumulate over lifetimes. However, these past traumas, called "engrams," limit the thetan's abilities and create emotional and mental barriers. By identifying and resolving these engrams through practices like auditing,

Scientologists aim to release the thetan from these limitations, allowing it to operate with greater awareness and freedom.

**Self-determination and autonomy are central qualities of the thetan**. Hubbard taught that the thetan is inherently capable of deciding its path and purpose. Unlike deterministic or materialistic perspectives, Scientology holds that the thetan has a will and purpose separate from the mind and body. This self-determination allows the thetan to shape its reality and destiny, making personal responsibility a cornerstone of Scientology practice. By acknowledging their power and responsibility as thetans, individuals can, according to Scientology, exercise greater control over their lives and futures.

The journey of self-discovery within Scientology is deeply tied to understanding oneself as a thetan. Auditing, a central practice in Scientology, helps individuals to confront and overcome the limitations imposed by past experiences, allowing the thetan to regain its native abilities. Scientologists believe that as they progress along the Bridge to Total Freedom—a structured path of spiritual advancement—they move closer to realizing their potential as spiritual beings. Each step along the Bridge is designed to increase the thetan's awareness, abilities, and freedom, ultimately aiming to restore its full capacities.

Hubbard also suggested that the thetan has perceptual abilities beyond those of the physical senses. Scientologists believe that the thetan can perceive things outside the physical spectrum, such as emotions, spiritual states, and intentions. This capacity for "exteriorization" is a unique aspect of Scientology's view of the spirit. Exteriorization refers to the thetan's ability to exist separate from the body, where it can observe and experience reality without physical constraints. For many Scientologists, achieving a sense of exteriorization is a profound experience, offering a direct realization of their nature as a thetan.

Hubbard's writings describe the thetan as inherently good, yet often hindered by negative experiences. In its natural state, the thetan is believed to possess qualities such as compassion, creativity, and the desire to help others. However, these qualities may become distorted over time due to accumulated traumas. Scientology's practices aim to "clear" these traumas, returning the thetan to a more natural, uninhibited state. Through this process, Scientologists believe they can gain clarity, overcome irrational fears, and strengthen their innate virtues.

Finally, the thetan's relationship to the **Eight Dynamics of Existence** is essential for understanding its role in life. The Eight Dynamics, which range from the self to all existence, guide the thetan's interactions with the world and other beings. Each dynamic represents a different aspect of life, encouraging Scientologists to consider how their spiritual self affects family, community, humanity, and beyond. The dynamics provide a framework for the thetan to balance personal development with a broader responsibility toward others and the universe. This holistic approach encourages the thetan to view life not as isolated but as interconnected with various forms of existence.

# The Eternal Nature of the Thetan

According to Scientology, the thetan's longevity stretches far beyond the lifespan of the human race or even the known universe. This belief positions the thetan as something separate from the material world, uninfluenced by the passage of time or the decay of the physical body. In practical terms, Scientologists view the thetan as constantly existing in an ongoing cycle of birth, death, and rebirth, inhabiting new bodies and experiencing new lives without ever losing its inherent nature. The continuity of existence, even through different lives, is fundamental to understanding the thetan's sense of self.

While the thetan may experience countless physical existences, these are seen as temporary conditions that do not alter its true nature. The body is viewed as a mere vessel, enabling the thetan to interact with the physical universe, but it doesn't define or limit the thetan's essence. In this context, each life is a new chapter, one in which the thetan takes on a fresh identity, relationships, and environment, but always with a sense of spiritual permanence. Scientologists believe that each life presents opportunities for growth, allowing the thetan to gain knowledge, confront challenges, and deepen its understanding.

Another aspect of the thetan's eternal nature is its resilience to physical death. Scientology teaches that while the body will inevitably age, become ill, and die, the thetan is unaffected by these changes. After a body's death, the thetan is free to move on, seeking a new life, new body, and new experiences. This ongoing cycle of rebirth reinforces the idea that the thetan's essence remains untouched by physical mortality. Each transition is seen as an opportunity to continue the journey of self-discovery and advancement, a continuous process with no final endpoint.

The thetan's timeless nature is central to Scientology's view of spiritual progress. Since the thetan spans multiple lives, it is believed to carry forward the impacts of past experiences, both positive and negative, into each new existence. This continuity explains why certain unresolved issues, fears, or limitations may persist across lifetimes. Auditing in Scientology is intended to address these influences by helping the thetan release burdens from previous lives, enabling it to move forward unencumbered in its current existence. This concept of past-life influences is crucial in Scientology's approach to freeing the thetan from old traumas.

Scientologists believe that understanding the thetan's eternal nature encourages a greater perspective on life. By recognizing themselves as timeless beings, individuals can reframe their lives as temporary stages in a much larger journey. This viewpoint influences decisions, priorities, and the value placed on spiritual growth over material concerns. For Scientologists, embracing the eternal nature of the thetan helps them to live with a sense of purpose, emphasizing personal responsibility and spiritual advancement over purely physical or material pursuits.

# The Relationship Between Thetan, Mind, and Body

Scientology holds that the thetan, mind, and body are distinct yet interdependent entities, each fulfilling a different role. The thetan is the spiritual core, the true self that directs both the mind and body but is not bound by either. In this framework, the body acts as the physical vehicle, allowing the thetan to engage with the physical world through sensory perception, movement, and action. The mind serves as the intermediary between the thetan and body, processing thoughts, emotions, memories, and experiences. This relationship allows the thetan to function in the material world, but without confusing itself with either the mind's thoughts or the body's sensations.

The body, in Scientology, is seen as an instrument that the thetan temporarily inhabits, using it to communicate, work, and navigate life's challenges. However, the body itself is viewed as a separate entity without independent consciousness; it relies on the thetan's direction to operate. This understanding emphasizes that physical sensations, desires, and even biological needs are related to the body, not the spiritual self. Scientologists believe that the thetan should maintain control over the body, rather than allowing physical urges or instincts to dictate its actions.

The mind acts as the interface between the spiritual and physical realms. Scientologists divide the mind into two parts: the **analytical mind** and the **reactive mind**. The analytical mind is logical, helping the thetan solve problems, process information, and make decisions based on rational thought. The reactive mind, on the other hand, stores negative experiences, fears, and emotional reactions in the form of engrams. These engrams can cloud the thetan's judgment and create automatic, irrational responses. Scientologists believe that by understanding and addressing the influences of the reactive mind, the thetan can regain control over its thoughts and actions, leading to greater clarity and peace.

The thetan's relationship with the mind is complex because, while the mind stores experiences and aids in decision-making, it can also hinder the thetan's ability to experience reality directly. Through auditing, Scientologists aim to clear engrams from the reactive mind, allowing the thetan to access a clearer, undistorted perception of life. In this process, the thetan reclaims control, using the analytical mind effectively while releasing the hold of past traumas. This helps the thetan maintain its own awareness and decision-making ability without being unduly influenced by the mind's stored responses.

**Exteriorization** is an important concept related to the thetan's relationship with the body and mind. Scientologists believe that through spiritual practices, the thetan can experience moments of exteriorization, where it feels separated from the body and views the world from an external perspective. This state reinforces the idea that the thetan is not bound by physical form and is capable of existing independently.

Exteriorization is often seen as a profound experience, offering the thetan direct insight into its true, non-physical nature and its separation from the mind and body.

Scientologists emphasize the need for the thetan to maintain mastery over both mind and body, avoiding becoming "effect" rather than "cause." This principle means that the thetan should act as the directing force, not passively responding to physical sensations or emotional triggers. By achieving a balanced relationship with the mind and body, the thetan can make conscious choices that align with its spiritual goals rather than reacting out of habit, fear, or past trauma. This dynamic approach is fundamental to Scientology's philosophy, emphasizing self-determination and awareness.

## The Role of the Thetan in Self-Improvement

In Scientology, self-improvement is a process led by the thetan, as it works to overcome limitations imposed by the mind and body. The thetan is considered inherently capable and aware, but it can become trapped or hindered by engrams and physical concerns. Scientology's approach to self-improvement focuses on helping the thetan regain control, clarity, and freedom to act according to its true intentions. The concept of self-improvement is deeply tied to the thetan's journey, as it works to reclaim its natural abilities and pursue a path toward spiritual enlightenment.

Self-improvement begins with identifying and confronting the thetan's reactive mind. Scientologists believe that the reactive mind stores painful experiences and traumas that cloud judgment and influence behavior. Through auditing, the thetan addresses these engrams, bringing them to consciousness and releasing their hold. This process is intended to free the thetan from the automatic, irrational responses associated with past traumas, enabling it to operate with greater self-control and rationality. In doing so, the thetan can actively work toward achieving a state of Clear, which is viewed as a significant milestone in the journey of self-improvement.

Once the thetan reaches Clear, its potential for self-improvement expands as it progresses through higher levels, known as **Operating Thetan (OT) levels**. These levels are designed to help the thetan further develop its awareness, skills, and insight. Each OT level provides specific exercises and practices that encourage the thetan to confront deeper spiritual challenges and increase its understanding of existence. For Scientologists, moving through OT levels represents a continuous path of self-improvement and discovery, helping the thetan gain abilities that transcend ordinary human experience.

Scientology also promotes personal growth through structured courses and training exercises, often referred to as **Training Routines (TRs)**. These routines are designed to enhance the thetan's ability to communicate effectively, maintain focus, and confront difficult situations without losing composure. TRs help the thetan build practical skills that support self-improvement in everyday life, reinforcing the idea that spiritual progress should translate into practical, observable benefits. By developing these skills, the thetan becomes better equipped to manage relationships, personal goals, and challenges.

As mentioned, scientologists believe that the thetan's role in self-improvement extends to the **Eight Dynamics**, encouraging personal growth not just for oneself but in areas that impact family, community, and humanity. Each dynamic represents an area of life where the thetan can strive for improvement, and Scientology teaches that true self-improvement involves expanding one's positive influence across all dynamics. This principle fosters a sense of responsibility toward others and the world, as the thetan works to bring harmony and ethical behavior into every area of life.

# CHAPTER 3: THE DYNAMICS OF EXISTENCE

## The First Dynamic: The Self

In Scientology, the First Dynamic—**the Self**—is the foundational element of the Eight Dynamics of Existence. It represents an individual's drive to survive and thrive as an independent, unique being. This dynamic is about self-preservation, personal goals, and understanding oneself as a thetan. Scientologists see the First Dynamic as the starting point of all awareness, growth, and achievement. The journey of spiritual development begins with understanding and improving the self, as one's actions and motivations are shaped by their individual identity, thoughts, and experiences.

The First Dynamic covers every aspect of a person's existence that is uniquely theirs: body, mind, spirit, and consciousness. Scientology teaches that each individual, or thetan, has the right and responsibility to care for themselves, to survive, and to succeed in life. This dynamic doesn't imply selfishness or isolation; rather, it encourages personal strength, resilience, and self-awareness as the foundation for further growth. In Scientology, self-improvement and spiritual advancement begin with a focus on this First Dynamic. By knowing oneself fully, the thetan can then address other dynamics in a balanced, effective way.

The concept of survival is key to the First Dynamic. According to Scientology, all life is driven by a basic impulse to survive, which influences every action and decision a person makes. This survival instinct includes not only physical well-being but also mental and spiritual health. By enhancing these aspects of survival, Scientologists believe individuals can lead more fulfilling and powerful lives. Auditing and self-reflection help individuals identify obstacles or negative patterns that may prevent them from fully thriving. The clearer the understanding of one's motivations, strengths, and weaknesses, the more effectively they can enhance their survival.

**Personal responsibility** is another essential part of the First Dynamic. Scientology teaches that each person is accountable for their own choices, actions, and outcomes. This accountability fosters a sense of autonomy and self-control, reinforcing that the thetan has the ability to shape their reality. Scientologists believe that acknowledging responsibility over one's own life is a critical step in spiritual growth. By recognizing the power of choice, individuals become more deliberate in their actions, working consciously toward goals that improve their own lives and, ultimately, the lives of others.

Self-awareness in the First Dynamic involves understanding the interplay between mind, body, and spirit. Scientology emphasizes that each part of a person's being should work in harmony to achieve maximum potential. The body is a vehicle, the mind is a tool for thought and memory, and the thetan is the true self. Scientology practices like auditing are designed to help individuals clear mental barriers or "engrams" that may interfere with this harmony. When these elements align, the individual can experience clarity, peace, and control over their own existence. This alignment is a central goal of Scientology, as it allows the thetan to operate freely without being held back by past traumas or reactive impulses.

The First Dynamic also encourages **self-determination**. Scientology views the self as an entity with the right to pursue its goals, beliefs, and values. This freedom, however, comes with the responsibility to use one's strengths wisely. For Scientologists, true self-determination means acting with integrity and purpose. It involves making choices that not only enhance one's survival but also align with their ethical standards. This is why the ethical guidelines in Scientology, like the Code of Honor, are so integral—they support individuals in staying true to their principles as they work to improve themselves.

In the First Dynamic, Scientologists are encouraged to set and pursue personal goals. These goals can range from improving one's physical health and emotional stability to gaining new skills or expanding knowledge. Scientology believes that when individuals focus on clear, meaningful objectives, they experience a sense of accomplishment and empowerment. Personal goals serve as a form of self-expression, allowing the thetan to shape their life in accordance with their unique desires and capacities. Achieving these goals is seen as a practical way to strengthen the First Dynamic, making the individual more effective and self-assured.

Lastly, the First Dynamic recognizes that self-care and self-respect are essential components of survival. Scientology encourages individuals to take actions that contribute to their well-being, whether through physical health, mental clarity, or spiritual awareness. Self-care isn't seen as indulgent but as necessary to support the other dynamics. By nurturing themselves, Scientologists believe they can contribute more meaningfully to family, groups, and society. This perspective aligns with the broader goal of Scientology: to create a world where individuals can be their best selves and work toward a more harmonious existence.

In Scientology, understanding and developing the First Dynamic is the basis of all personal and spiritual growth. It's seen as the starting point from which individuals can build a balanced, ethical, and purpose-driven life.


## The Second Dynamic: Family and Relationships

The Second Dynamic in Scientology focuses on **family, reproduction, and relationships**, extending the principle of survival from the individual to one's close personal connections. Scientologists view this dynamic as encompassing all aspects of family life and relationships, including marriage, parenthood, friendship, and any bond that promotes personal and collective survival. Scientology holds that strong, supportive relationships are crucial for spiritual and emotional well-being, and that the family unit is central to the stability of both individuals and society as a whole.

Central to the Second Dynamic is the idea of **creating and nurturing future generations**. Scientology teaches that procreation and raising children are vital contributions to survival, as they ensure the continuity of life and values. This dynamic emphasizes that parents have a responsibility to guide, support, and educate their children to become ethical, competent individuals. Scientologists believe that a stable family environment allows children to grow up with a sense of security, purpose, and self-worth. Children, in turn, are viewed as the future of the community, and providing them with a solid foundation is considered a key responsibility of every parent.

**Marriage is an important component of the Second Dynamic**. In Scientology, marriage is not only a personal commitment but also a partnership that supports spiritual goals and mutual respect. Scientologists see marriage as a union that should help both partners reach higher states of spiritual awareness and ethical living. Couples are encouraged to support each other's spiritual paths and maintain harmony within the household. The Church of Scientology provides courses and counseling services aimed at helping couples improve communication, resolve conflicts, and strengthen their relationships, viewing these as essential to the family's overall survival and well-being.

Scientology also stresses **personal responsibility within relationships**. The Second Dynamic teaches that each person has a duty to contribute positively to their family and close relationships. This responsibility includes acting with integrity, resolving conflicts constructively, and supporting one another's goals. Scientologists believe that individuals should take an active role in improving their relationships by handling personal issues that could negatively impact the family. Techniques like auditing and communication drills are offered to help Scientologists address personal barriers that may affect their relationships, enabling them to create a stable, supportive family environment.

**Friendship and extended relationships** also fall within the Second Dynamic, as these connections impact an individual's immediate support system. While family is the primary focus, Scientology recognizes the importance of forming bonds with friends and mentors who share similar values and contribute to one's well-being. These relationships can provide emotional support, collaboration, and encouragement in times of difficulty, enhancing the individual's survival. Scientologists are encouraged to develop friendships based on mutual respect and shared goals, building a network that aligns with their personal and spiritual aspirations.

**Education within the family** is emphasized as a critical part of the Second Dynamic. Scientologists believe that teaching children ethical values, responsibility, and effective communication lays the groundwork for future stability. Parents are encouraged to pass on the principles they have learned in Scientology, fostering a sense of integrity and purpose in their children. By instilling these values early,

Scientologists believe they are helping create a generation that will contribute positively to society and uphold the principles of Scientology.

## The Third and Fourth Dynamics: Groups and Mankind

The Third and Fourth Dynamics in Scientology expand the focus from individual survival and family to **social and global survival**. The Third Dynamic covers groups, organizations, and communities, while the Fourth Dynamic extends to humanity as a whole. These dynamics reflect the belief that survival and growth are interconnected with larger social structures, and that one's actions should benefit not only the self and family but also society and humanity. Scientologists see participation in these broader dynamics as essential to contributing to a stable, ethical world.

The **Third Dynamic** refers to the collective groups that people participate in throughout life. This includes workplaces, social clubs, teams, religious congregations, and other organizations. Scientologists believe that groups help individuals expand their influence, resources, and knowledge, contributing to survival on a larger scale. The Church of Scientology encourages members to engage with groups that align with their values and to take an active role in promoting ethical behavior within those groups. By participating responsibly, Scientologists believe they can improve the overall quality and harmony of their environment, making it more conducive to spiritual growth.

A key aspect of the Third Dynamic is the principle of **group ethics**. Scientologists view each group as having a shared purpose and a set of ethics to guide its members. When individuals contribute to their groups ethically, they help create stability, cooperation, and productivity within that group. The Church of Scientology offers courses and auditing specifically aimed at helping members improve their effectiveness within groups. These practices encourage clear communication, accountability, and personal responsibility, which are seen as vital for a group's survival and success. The aim is to foster a culture where individuals support each other's growth and contribute positively to collective goals.

Scientologists are also encouraged to **address conflicts within groups constructively**. Through communication techniques and conflict-resolution tools, Scientology teaches members to confront and resolve disagreements effectively. The focus is on creating win-win situations that benefit both the individual and the group, avoiding behaviors that could harm group stability. By managing conflicts and promoting open communication, Scientologists believe they can contribute to a more ethical and supportive group environment, benefiting both their immediate social circles and the wider community.

The **Fourth Dynamic**, which encompasses all of humanity, represents an even broader level of survival. This dynamic emphasizes that individuals are part of the global human family and have a responsibility to contribute positively to humanity's well-being. Scientologists believe that their actions should support not only their own lives and groups but also the entire human race. The Church promotes this perspective by encouraging members to participate in humanitarian efforts, such as drug rehabilitation, criminal reform, and literacy programs, aimed at improving societal conditions.

One of the Fourth Dynamic's key elements is the concept of **"Clearing the Planet."** In Scientology, this term refers to the goal of creating a world where individuals are free from the limitations of the reactive mind. By advancing toward this ideal, Scientologists believe they can help eliminate crime, violence, and suffering. "Clearing the Planet" is seen as a responsibility shared by all Scientologists, each working toward a more ethical and spiritually aware society. This mission underpins many of the Church's social programs and outreach efforts, which aim to address issues that Scientologists believe hinder humanity's collective survival.

Scientologists are also taught to respect diversity within the Fourth Dynamic. Although the Church advocates for its own methods and philosophy, it recognizes the importance of cultural and religious diversity. This respect aligns with the belief that humanity benefits from various perspectives, and that constructive engagement with different communities contributes to the Fourth Dynamic's overall survival.

Through the Third and Fourth Dynamics, Scientologists aim to impact both their immediate social groups and the broader human population. By working within these dynamics, they believe they are expanding their purpose beyond personal concerns, contributing to the survival and advancement of society and humanity.

## The Eighth Dynamic and the Concept of Infinity

The Eighth Dynamic in Scientology refers to the ultimate, all-encompassing level of existence: **infinity** or the concept of a Supreme Being. This dynamic represents the culmination of all existence, transcending individual and collective levels to include the entirety of the universe and beyond. Scientologists are encouraged to explore and understand this dynamic as a way to reach the deepest level of spiritual awareness. The Eighth Dynamic embodies an individual's relationship with the infinite, the spiritual, and the unknown, where traditional concepts of time, space, and matter fall away, leaving only the pursuit of ultimate understanding.

In Scientology, the Eighth Dynamic is not strictly defined. L. Ron Hubbard described it as the "dynamic of infinity," allowing each person to interpret it based on their own experiences and beliefs. Some view it as a recognition of God, a higher power, or a divine essence that pervades all existence. Others may see it as an abstract concept representing ultimate truth or cosmic order. This openness reflects Scientology's approach to spirituality, encouraging individuals to find their own meaning within the Eighth Dynamic while still viewing it as an essential part of the journey toward enlightenment.

The Eighth Dynamic is distinct from other dynamics because it is not centered on material survival or social relationships. Instead, it focuses on spiritual survival, aiming to understand what lies beyond physical and worldly concerns. Scientologists see this dynamic as a way to explore questions of existence and purpose, moving beyond immediate concerns to contemplate life's broader meaning. This dynamic invites each person to consider their place in the universe and the interconnectedness of all existence. Through this exploration, Scientologists believe they can gain a greater sense of harmony with themselves, others, and the cosmos.

**Awareness of the Eighth Dynamic** often influences how Scientologists approach other areas of life. When individuals understand themselves as part of an infinite existence, they may be more inclined to act ethically, show compassion, and make choices that reflect their spiritual beliefs. The Eighth Dynamic encourages a perspective that reaches beyond individual or collective gain, fostering a sense of universal responsibility. By aligning with this dynamic, Scientologists believe they can contribute positively to their communities and the world, seeing their actions as part of a larger spiritual mission.

In Scientology practices, the Eighth Dynamic becomes especially significant at advanced levels of training and processing. As individuals progress through the OT (Operating Thetan) levels, they are encouraged to expand their awareness, seeking to understand their own spiritual nature in the context of infinity. This process involves not only reflecting on one's own existence but also contemplating the broader questions of life and the universe. Through these levels, Scientologists believe they are developing a direct connection with the Eighth Dynamic, moving closer to an understanding of ultimate truth.

While the Eighth Dynamic encourages each person to seek their understanding of infinity, Scientology also offers structured guidance through teachings, exercises, and spiritual processing. This structured approach aims to help individuals reach a state where they feel a deep connection to the infinite, or to whatever they define as their highest spiritual reality. Scientologists see this connection as essential for achieving spiritual freedom and clarity, believing that the Eighth Dynamic helps them transcend ordinary experiences and move into realms of heightened perception.

The Eighth Dynamic is seen as a unifying force that connects all other dynamics. It provides a context in which each individual can explore not only their place in the world but their role within the entire scope of existence. For many Scientologists, the Eighth Dynamic is a personal journey toward understanding their spiritual identity in relation to an infinite universe. Whether defined as God, ultimate truth, or cosmic oneness, the Eighth Dynamic represents the highest level of awareness and self-realization that Scientology encourages individuals to strive for.

# Balancing All Eight Dynamics for Holistic Growth

Scientology teaches that **balancing all Eight Dynamics** is essential for a well-rounded, fulfilling life. Each dynamic represents a different aspect of existence, from the self (First Dynamic) to family, groups, mankind, living things, the physical universe, spirituality, and finally infinity. Scientologists believe that focusing on only one or two dynamics leads to an unbalanced life, as each dynamic is interconnected. Achieving holistic growth means developing each dynamic in a way that complements the others, ensuring a harmonious approach to both personal and spiritual well-being.

The balance begins with the **First Dynamic—the self**—where individuals focus on understanding their own needs, goals, and personal development. Scientologists believe that a strong sense of self-awareness and personal responsibility lays the foundation for balancing the other dynamics. If a person neglects the First Dynamic, they may struggle to engage meaningfully with family, groups, or society. This emphasis on self-responsibility encourages individuals to address their mental, physical, and spiritual needs first, so they can contribute effectively to the other dynamics.

In the **Second Dynamic**, which encompasses family and relationships, Scientologists see balance as nurturing bonds with loved ones while respecting personal goals. The Second Dynamic highlights the importance of building strong, supportive relationships, especially with family members. However, Scientology teaches that family obligations should not dominate one's life to the point of neglecting self-growth or community involvement. Balancing the Second Dynamic means actively participating in family life while maintaining individual boundaries and personal aspirations, aligning with broader ethical values.

The **Third Dynamic** focuses on groups, such as workplaces, teams, or communities. Scientologists believe that effective group participation requires a blend of loyalty, accountability, and independence. Balancing this dynamic involves contributing positively to groups without compromising one's principles. A person who is too absorbed in group activities might lose sight of individual goals, while someone who avoids groups may miss out on the benefits of collective effort and cooperation. Scientology encourages members to find a role within groups where they can express their abilities while supporting the group's success, achieving a synergy between individual and collective aims.

The **Fourth Dynamic—mankind as a whole**—invites Scientologists to consider their role in the human family. Here, balance means contributing to humanity's welfare through ethical actions, community service, or humanitarian work. This dynamic extends beyond local or national boundaries, promoting a global outlook. However, Scientologists are taught to balance this broad perspective with personal and group responsibilities. In other words, a balanced Fourth Dynamic does not mean losing sight of family, group, or self while trying to improve the world; rather, it's about making meaningful contributions to humanity that don't overshadow other dynamics.

The **Fifth and Sixth Dynamics** cover all life forms and the physical universe. Balancing these dynamics involves respecting and understanding the interconnectedness of all life, from animals and plants to the natural environment. Scientologists are encouraged to act in ways that support environmental well-being and sustainability, recognizing that the physical universe is the shared space in which all dynamics exist. However, prioritizing environmental concerns without consideration for family, group, or self would be imbalanced. Scientology's view of these dynamics promotes a relationship with nature that is respectful and mindful, without neglecting the other aspects of existence.

The **Seventh Dynamic—spirituality**—is where Scientologists explore their connection with the spiritual world, independent of the physical universe. Achieving balance here means pursuing personal spiritual growth without isolating oneself from the practical aspects of life. While Scientology encourages members to seek higher spiritual awareness, they are also taught to integrate these insights into their daily lives. A person deeply focused on spirituality but disconnected from family or community may struggle to achieve balance. Thus, Scientologists are encouraged to let their spiritual insights guide their actions across all dynamics, ensuring that their spiritual growth positively impacts family, groups, and society.

Finally, the **Eighth Dynamic—Infinity or the Supreme Being**—is the overarching dynamic that connects all other areas of existence. Scientologists see this dynamic as representing ultimate spiritual awareness and the pursuit of an understanding of infinity. Balancing the Eighth Dynamic involves integrating a sense of universal responsibility and awareness without losing touch with everyday responsibilities. When individuals recognize their role within the infinite, they gain a broader perspective that informs their interactions with others, their approach to challenges, and their ethical decisions. However, balance in the Eighth Dynamic doesn't mean retreating entirely into abstract spirituality; rather, it means allowing a sense of purpose to permeate actions in all other dynamics.

# CHAPTER 4: THE MIND AND SCIENTOLOGY

## The Analytical Mind vs. the Reactive Mind

In Scientology, the mind is divided into two parts: the **analytical mind** and the **reactive mind**. Each serves a distinct purpose, with unique functions that influence thought, behavior, and decision-making. Understanding the differences between these two minds is fundamental to Scientology, as this knowledge forms the basis for auditing, personal growth, and mental clarity.

The **analytical mind** is the rational, conscious part of the mind. It processes information logically, evaluating facts, making calculations, and solving problems. In Scientology, the analytical mind is described as being similar to a computer, constantly gathering and processing data from the environment. When functioning properly, it enables individuals to make clear, reasoned decisions based on observed reality. For instance, when someone drives a car, their analytical mind processes factors like speed, distance, and traffic to keep them safe and aware. This part of the mind is fully awake and alert, engaged in thinking critically and planning actions.

**The analytical mind operates in the present**, considering past experiences and knowledge without being overly influenced by them. It works with memories and observations, using them as data points rather than as triggers for emotional responses. For example, if a person remembers a past failure, the analytical mind assesses it as information rather than as a reason to feel fear or guilt. The goal of the analytical mind is to help individuals approach life with clarity, applying reasoning rather than automatic reactions to situations. Scientologists view this mind as essential for effective functioning and survival, as it helps people respond to their environment in a balanced, intelligent way.

In contrast, the **reactive mind** operates differently. The reactive mind is **non-rational and emotional**, and it stores painful or traumatic experiences as "engrams." These engrams are memories of distressing incidents, often accompanied by intense feelings or physical pain. Unlike the analytical mind, which analyzes and interprets information, the reactive mind records these moments without filtering them, reacting automatically whenever similar situations arise. If, for instance, someone was in a car accident, the reactive mind might store the sounds, smells, and sensations associated with the event. Later, hearing a loud noise similar to the one from the accident could trigger feelings of fear or panic, even if there's no actual danger.

**The reactive mind operates on a stimulus-response basis**. It reacts to certain "triggers," or reminders of past traumas, with pre-programmed emotional responses. These reactions are not based on rational thought; instead, they're automatic and often disruptive. The reactive mind doesn't analyze or question; it simply responds. Scientologists believe that these automatic reactions can interfere with daily life, causing individuals to act in ways that don't align with their true desires or logic. For example, someone might avoid social situations because of a traumatic experience, even though they rationally want to engage with others. The reactive mind's influence is seen as limiting, as it pulls a person away from their analytical mind's logical approach.

Scientology teaches that **engrams in the reactive mind accumulate over time**, becoming mental and emotional barriers that affect one's behavior and mental health. Each engram carries with it the emotions and physical sensations of the original incident, replaying these feelings whenever they're triggered. As these engrams pile up, they can cloud a person's perspective, leading to irrational fears, anxiety, and even physical symptoms. This process is often unconscious, as the reactive mind operates beneath the surface, without the person's active awareness. Scientologists view these stored traumas as obstacles to self-improvement and spiritual freedom, as they prevent individuals from fully engaging with life in a calm, clear-headed way.

To address the influence of the reactive mind, Scientology employs **auditing**, a practice aimed at identifying and clearing engrams. During auditing, an individual works with an auditor to recall and re-experience past traumatic incidents. By confronting these memories, they can release the emotional and mental charge associated with them, reducing the reactive mind's influence. The goal is to free the individual from automatic, irrational reactions, allowing the analytical mind to operate without interference. Scientologists believe that as engrams are cleared, the person becomes more "Clear," with the analytical mind fully in control.

Scientology's view of the **analytical vs. reactive mind** underscores its approach to personal responsibility and self-determination. The analytical mind represents an individual's conscious choices and logical thought, while the reactive mind symbolizes automatic, involuntary responses rooted in past pain. By learning to recognize and address the reactive mind's influence, Scientologists aim to achieve greater self-awareness, freedom, and control over their own actions and emotions. This separation between analytical and reactive minds is central to Scientology's teachings, as it provides a pathway to mental clarity and spiritual progress.

## The Engram: Source of Mental and Emotional Pain

In Scientology, **engrams** are defined as memories of painful or traumatic incidents that become stored in the reactive mind. These engrams act as mental and emotional barriers, affecting a person's responses, feelings, and even physical health. Scientologists believe that engrams are not merely memories but recordings of all sensory perceptions tied to the incident, including sounds, smells, physical sensations, and emotions. These memories are stored deeply and involuntarily, often without the individual's conscious awareness, and they resurface when triggered, causing irrational reactions that can impact every dynamic of existence.

Engrams are seen as sources of **mental and emotional pain** because they embed unresolved negative experiences within the mind, waiting to be triggered in future situations. For instance, if someone experiences an intense moment of fear during a car accident, the reactive mind might store the sensations of that moment as an engram. Later, a similar sensation, like the sound of screeching tires, can activate the engram, causing fear and anxiety—even if the person is no longer in any real danger. These responses bypass the analytical mind, leading to automatic reactions that can interfere with day-to-day life and hinder progress in personal, family, and social dynamics.

Scientology views engrams as **barriers to survival** across all dynamics. By influencing behavior and emotions, engrams can harm relationships, affect group involvement, and limit one's capacity to contribute positively to society. If left unresolved, engrams can create a pattern of behavior where individuals react emotionally rather than rationally, potentially harming both themselves and others. Scientologists believe that by confronting and clearing these engrams through auditing, a person can gain freedom from irrational reactions and achieve greater control over their own mind, ultimately enhancing their ability to contribute meaningfully to all dynamics.

The process of **storing and activating engrams** is central to understanding Scientology's approach to mental health. Scientologists believe that engrams are recorded when the analytical mind is bypassed, such as during moments of intense pain, stress, or unconsciousness. During these moments, the reactive mind takes control, recording the incident in detail. The engram then lies dormant until a similar situation arises, triggering the stored response. This mechanism can create a cycle of pain and avoidance, where the individual repeatedly reacts to situations based on past traumas rather than current realities. Scientologists view this cycle as limiting, as it prevents individuals from fully engaging with life and making rational, intentional choices.

In addressing engrams, Scientology aims to **restore mental clarity** and improve well-being across all dynamics. By identifying and confronting these engrams in auditing, a person can reduce the influence of the reactive mind and enable the analytical mind to operate without interference. This process is viewed as essential for achieving a state of "Clear," where the individual is no longer controlled by past traumas. Reaching this state is seen as a major step in personal and spiritual development, as it frees the individual to interact with others, participate in groups, and contribute to society without the constraints of irrational fears or emotional pain.


## Mechanisms of the Mind: How it Affects Actions and Choices

Scientology views the mind as a complex system that influences a person's actions, decisions, and ability to engage effectively with each dynamic. The **analytical mind** and the **reactive mind** work together, though often at odds, shaping the ways individuals think, feel, and behave. While the analytical mind processes information rationally, helping individuals make logical decisions, the reactive mind introduces automatic responses based on past experiences. Scientologists believe that these mechanisms affect all areas of existence, as the mind's structure and function have a direct role in shaping behavior, relationships, and overall survival.

The **analytical mind** is responsible for evaluating current circumstances, drawing on experience, and solving problems in real time. This part of the mind operates consciously, gathering data, assessing options, and considering outcomes. When a person functions primarily through the analytical mind, they can approach life with reason and intention, making decisions that align with their goals in each dynamic —whether in personal, family, group, or societal matters. For example, an individual might weigh the pros and cons of a job opportunity by considering its impact on their family and personal well-being. This approach promotes thoughtful decision-making that aligns with both immediate and long-term objectives.

The **reactive mind**, however, introduces automatic responses, often based on past trauma or stress. When an individual encounters a trigger—a sensation, sound, or situation reminiscent of a painful past experience—the reactive mind takes control, influencing behavior without conscious awareness. For example, someone who faced rejection in a social setting might automatically withdraw in similar situations, even if they consciously want to engage. Scientologists see these responses as limitations on personal freedom and success in each dynamic, as they prevent individuals from acting in their best interest.

The reactive mind operates **outside of rational thought**, which can lead to choices that are counterproductive or even harmful. The irrational responses triggered by the reactive mind can manifest as fear, anger, or avoidance, impacting relationships, work, and group participation. These reactions, driven by unresolved engrams, interfere with logical decision-making and cause individuals to repeat negative patterns, limiting growth and positive engagement across dynamics. Scientology's auditing process addresses these engrams by helping individuals bring these memories to consciousness, enabling them to examine and release the emotional charge, thus restoring the analytical mind's control.

Scientologists believe that **addressing the mechanisms of the mind** leads to more deliberate, beneficial choices. By clearing the reactive mind of engrams, individuals gain the freedom to act thoughtfully in all dynamics—without past traumas clouding their judgment. This freedom supports a balanced life, where each dynamic is nurtured with awareness and responsibility. When individuals make decisions without interference from the reactive mind, they can focus on positive relationships, effective group interactions, and contributing to society, achieving a sense of purpose and fulfillment.

The **mind's influence extends across all eight dynamics**, affecting how individuals relate to themselves, their families, and the larger world. Scientology's focus on clearing engrams and restoring the analytical mind's function is seen as crucial for enabling each person to fulfill their potential within these dynamics. As individuals work to resolve the reactive mind's influence, they gain the ability to act in ways that promote survival, growth, and well-being in every area of their lives.

## The Importance of Mental Clarity in Scientology

In Scientology, **mental clarity** is fundamental to thriving within each dynamic of existence. Mental clarity allows the analytical mind to function optimally, free from the interference of the reactive mind's stored engrams. Scientologists believe that achieving mental clarity empowers individuals to engage fully with life, make rational decisions, and interact positively across all dynamics—from personal development to family, groups, and society. When the mind operates clearly, individuals are better equipped to understand themselves, navigate relationships, and contribute to society with intention and purpose.

Mental clarity enables individuals to approach each dynamic with awareness and focus. In the First Dynamic, the self, clarity allows a person to identify their goals, strengths, and areas for improvement without being clouded by irrational fears or insecurities. This self-understanding is the basis for growth, as it allows individuals to address personal challenges head-on. In the context of family and relationships, mental clarity supports open communication and rational conflict resolution, reducing the likelihood of misunderstandings or reactive behaviors that can harm bonds. When the mind is clear, individuals can act in ways that strengthen relationships, support their families, and foster a stable home environment.

In group dynamics, clarity of mind enhances cooperation and accountability. Scientologists believe that by reducing reactive responses, individuals can better assess group goals, understand their role, and work effectively with others. A clear mind enables people to approach group interactions with maturity and respect, avoiding conflicts rooted in unresolved personal issues. In the workplace, this clarity supports productivity and ethical conduct, as it enables people to approach tasks with focus and professionalism. Scientologists see these qualities as essential for contributing to the success of groups and organizations within the Third Dynamic.

In the broader scope of humanity and society—the Fourth Dynamic—mental clarity encourages ethical, thoughtful engagement. When individuals are free from reactive impulses, they are better able to consider the impact of their actions on others and make choices that align with humanitarian values. For Scientologists, clarity in the Fourth Dynamic fosters an approach to life that is both compassionate and rational, promoting social harmony and collective well-being. A clear mind enables people to contribute positively to humanity, recognizing their role in shaping a world where ethical values and survival are aligned.

Mental clarity is also essential for **spiritual awareness** in the higher dynamics, particularly the Seventh and Eighth Dynamics, which encompass spirituality and infinity. Scientologists believe that unresolved engrams and irrational fears block spiritual perception and understanding. Achieving clarity allows individuals to explore spiritual truths without interference from past experiences, leading to a deeper connection with their spiritual self and the universe. For Scientologists, this clear-minded approach to spirituality brings a sense of purpose that transcends the material world, enhancing their journey toward self-discovery and enlightenment.

From pursuing mental clarity through auditing and other practices, Scientologists aim to remove mental and emotional obstacles that limit growth in all aspects of life. With a clear mind, they believe they can engage fully with each dynamic, making choices that support survival, personal development, and positive contributions to family, society, and beyond.

# CHAPTER 5: THE BRIDGE TO TOTAL FREEDOM

## The Purpose of the Bridge

The **Bridge to Total Freedom** in Scientology is a structured path designed to guide individuals toward achieving spiritual awareness, mental clarity, and ultimately, a state of complete freedom as a thetan. This Bridge serves as a roadmap for personal and spiritual development, offering specific steps for individuals to follow as they progress. Each stage on the Bridge introduces practices and insights that address different aspects of the mind, spirit, and existence. Scientologists believe that by following the Bridge, a person can gradually free themselves from the limitations imposed by the reactive mind, accumulated traumas, and other barriers that inhibit spiritual growth.

The **purpose of the Bridge** is to help individuals reach their full potential by systematically addressing and clearing the obstacles that cloud their awareness and restrict their abilities. The ultimate goal is to become fully aware as a spiritual being, free from the mental and emotional limitations that influence behavior and perception. The Bridge is structured to start with the foundational aspects of mental clarity and self-understanding and move progressively toward more advanced levels of spiritual awareness. Each level on the Bridge builds on the last, allowing Scientologists to gain deeper insights and more profound control over their lives as they advance.

A significant part of the Bridge is **achieving the state of Clear**. In Scientology, a Clear is someone who has successfully rid themselves of the reactive mind, which contains engrams—painful or traumatic memories stored in a part of the mind that triggers irrational responses. By reaching Clear, an individual is no longer affected by these stored traumas and can approach life with full rationality and control. This state is seen as a critical milestone on the Bridge, as it provides a foundation for further spiritual exploration. Scientologists view achieving Clear as a transformative moment, allowing them to move past mental obstacles and begin focusing on the spiritual aspects of their journey.

After reaching Clear, the Bridge introduces the **Operating Thetan (OT) levels**, which focus on increasing spiritual awareness and abilities beyond the physical world. The OT levels are designed to help individuals understand their true identity as a thetan and their relationship with the universe. Through these levels, Scientologists seek to expand their perception, uncover new spiritual abilities, and gain a deeper connection to the Eight Dynamics of existence. The OT levels encourage practitioners to explore their awareness beyond immediate surroundings and recognize their role within the larger scope of life and the universe.

The purpose of the Bridge is also to provide **structure and guidance** for self-improvement. Each step is clearly defined, giving Scientologists a specific set of practices, objectives, and achievements to work toward. This structure allows individuals to see their progress in concrete terms, helping them stay motivated and focused on their goals. Scientologists believe that this organized approach allows for consistent, measurable development, preventing individuals from becoming overwhelmed or aimless in their spiritual journey. By following the Bridge, they can see a clear path toward self-realization and freedom, which encourages persistence and commitment.

A unique aspect of the Bridge is its focus on **personal responsibility and ethics**. As individuals progress, they're encouraged to take greater responsibility for their actions, decisions, and the impact they have on others. This responsibility is seen as essential for spiritual growth, as it aligns a person's behavior with their true nature as a thetan. The Bridge emphasizes ethical behavior and personal integrity, as these qualities are thought to support mental and spiritual freedom. Scientologists view the Bridge as a path to becoming not just more aware, but also more ethical, compassionate, and respectful of life.

Another purpose of the Bridge is to **empower individuals to address all areas of life** effectively. By working through each stage, a person develops tools and insights that enhance their ability to handle relationships, work, personal challenges, and social responsibilities. Scientology teaches that achieving spiritual freedom should not isolate a person from the world but rather enhance their capacity to engage meaningfully with it. Scientologists see the Bridge as a means of equipping themselves with practical skills that improve their quality of life, enabling them to be better partners, parents, leaders, and community members. In this way, the Bridge is both a personal and a social journey.

Throughout the Bridge, Scientologists are encouraged to **actively participate in the process of their own growth**, rather than passively seeking enlightenment. Auditing, training, and other practices on the Bridge are meant to be interactive, with individuals engaging fully in their journey. This active participation is thought to foster self-confidence, resilience, and an enduring sense of empowerment. By taking ownership of their spiritual path, Scientologists aim to reach a state of independence and inner peace that they believe is the hallmark of true freedom.

## Key Levels and Steps on the Bridge

The **Bridge to Total Freedom** is organized into a series of key levels and steps, each designed to address specific aspects of mental and spiritual development. The Bridge provides a structured path that guides Scientologists through increasingly advanced levels of understanding and control over their lives. Every step on the Bridge has a unique purpose and set of goals, enabling practitioners to confront and overcome different barriers on their journey to spiritual freedom.

The first levels of the Bridge focus on **personal awareness and overcoming the reactive mind**. In these initial stages, individuals engage in auditing processes that help them address engrams, or painful memories stored in the reactive mind. Through auditing, they aim to release these mental and emotional burdens, bringing them closer to the state of Clear. Early on, individuals also complete training courses to develop practical skills, such as effective communication and self-discipline, which are essential for progressing smoothly through the later stages of the Bridge.

One of the most important levels on the Bridge is **Clear**, a state in which the individual has freed themselves from the reactive mind. Achieving Clear is seen as a significant breakthrough, as it allows a person to function without the automatic, irrational responses tied to past traumas. Clear is not the end, however—it is considered a foundation for the more advanced levels of spiritual growth that follow. At Clear, individuals have greater mental clarity, emotional stability, and control over their thoughts and actions, making them better prepared to address the higher spiritual dimensions that lie ahead on the Bridge.

After reaching Clear, Scientologists begin advancing through the **Operating Thetan (OT) levels**, which form the upper levels of the Bridge. These OT levels focus on the spiritual aspects of existence, guiding individuals to explore their nature as thetans and their relationship with the universe. Each OT level addresses different challenges and areas of awareness, encouraging Scientologists to expand their spiritual insight and discover latent abilities. For instance, OT I introduces individuals to heightened levels of self-perception, while OT III explores deeper layers of existence beyond the physical realm.

The OT levels progressively build upon each other, with each stage offering unique experiences and insights. **OT VIII**, the highest level currently available, is regarded as a pinnacle of spiritual achievement in Scientology. At this stage, individuals are believed to have reached a profound understanding of their spiritual identity and a clear perception of the dynamics of existence. Reaching OT VIII is seen as a significant accomplishment, symbolizing a high degree of spiritual freedom and awareness.

In addition to auditing levels, the Bridge includes **training steps that focus on developing auditing skills**. Scientology believes that learning to audit others enhances one's understanding of the mind and spirit, reinforcing personal growth. By training to become an auditor, Scientologists learn to guide others through the same processes that helped them, deepening their own insights in the process. This training is viewed as an essential part of the Bridge, as it encourages individuals to support each other's journeys toward freedom.

The Bridge also includes specialized courses in **ethics and personal responsibility**. These courses help individuals align their actions with Scientology's ethical standards, ensuring that they act in ways that support their spiritual development. Ethics steps on the Bridge encourage self-reflection and accountability, fostering behaviors that align with survival and constructive engagement in each dynamic of existence. By strengthening personal integrity, Scientologists believe they can maintain the clarity and freedom achieved at each level.

Each step on the Bridge is designed to be progressive, building upon the successes of previous levels. This structure allows individuals to gain skills and knowledge that prepare them for more challenging levels. **Consistency and dedication** are encouraged, as the Bridge's levels are intended to be followed in sequence to ensure comprehensive growth. Scientologists view the Bridge as a complete system for achieving mental clarity, ethical awareness, and spiritual freedom.

## Moving from Pre-Clear to Clear Status

In Scientology, **moving from Pre-Clear to Clear** is a transformative journey that signifies a fundamental shift in an individual's mental and spiritual state. Pre-Clear refers to someone who has begun the auditing process but has not yet reached the state of Clear. This person is in the early stages of addressing the influence of the reactive mind, with its engrams and automatic responses, and is working toward a level of self-awareness and control that Clear represents.

At the Pre-Clear stage, individuals are **guided through auditing sessions** to confront and release engrams. Auditing is a central practice that involves revisiting past experiences stored in the reactive mind, particularly those associated with pain, fear, or trauma. These sessions aim to bring these experiences to consciousness, allowing the Pre-Clear to process them and remove the emotional charge they carry. As engrams are cleared, the individual's reactive mind loses its power, reducing the influence of automatic, irrational responses in daily life. This clearing process allows Pre-Clears to experience moments of mental clarity and rational thinking that build a foundation for reaching Clear.

Throughout this journey, the Pre-Clear gains a **growing sense of self-control**. As engrams are identified and processed, individuals find themselves less affected by triggers that previously caused emotional reactions. This improved mental stability is seen as essential for the Pre-Clear, enabling them to handle relationships, work situations, and other dynamics with greater calm and insight. Scientologists believe that by gaining control over these responses, Pre-Clears can begin to approach life with greater intentionality and rationality.

An important part of moving from Pre-Clear to Clear is the **commitment to self-improvement and personal responsibility**. Scientology teaches that each person is responsible for addressing their own mind, acknowledging the impact of the reactive mind on their behavior, and taking active steps to reach mental clarity. This commitment drives Pre-Clears to actively engage with the auditing process, understanding that each session brings them closer to freedom from mental and emotional limitations. Personal responsibility is viewed as the foundation of achieving Clear, as it ensures that individuals take ownership of their journey.

The experience of **achieving Clear** is described as a moment of liberation from the reactive mind's influence. At Clear, individuals are no longer affected by engrams, meaning they can make decisions based solely on present circumstances without interference from past traumas. The freedom from automatic responses enables Clears to experience life with a new sense of peace, stability, and purpose. They are better equipped to handle relationships, career challenges, and personal goals, as they now operate from a place of mental clarity rather than unconscious reactions. Scientologists view Clear as the beginning of a higher state of existence, where the mind operates as a tool under the thetan's control rather than an obstacle.

Once a person reaches Clear, they gain **access to the higher levels of the Bridge**. While Clear represents freedom from the reactive mind, the OT (Operating Thetan) levels introduce individuals to spiritual challenges beyond the mind. Moving forward, Clears explore their identity as thetans, gradually expanding their awareness of spiritual dimensions. Clear is seen as a milestone that opens the door to deeper levels of understanding and ability, marking the transition from mental freedom to spiritual exploration.

The journey from Pre-Clear to Clear is intended to create a solid foundation for the rest of the Bridge. By achieving Clear, Scientologists believe individuals gain a sense of liberation and empowerment that enables them to continue their spiritual journey with clarity and purpose. This transition is viewed not only as a personal victory but as the beginning of a new, conscious way of living.

## Achieving Freedom from Limitations

On the **Bridge to Total Freedom**, achieving freedom from limitations is a central goal, marking progress toward a state where an individual is no longer constrained by past traumas, irrational fears, or automatic responses. Scientologists believe that mental and emotional barriers—primarily those rooted in the reactive mind—limit a person's true potential and affect every aspect of life. These limitations stem from engrams, or deeply stored memories of painful experiences, which create automatic responses that override logical thought. Scientology teaches that by moving through the Bridge, individuals systematically confront and release these limitations, gradually reclaiming control over their minds and actions.

The **clearing process** in Scientology is designed specifically to address these barriers. Through auditing, a person identifies and processes engrams, which helps lessen the reactive mind's hold over them. This process is intended to free them from the involuntary reactions that previously dictated their responses to stress, conflict, and other challenges. As these limitations are released, individuals gain increased mental clarity and emotional stability, which allow them to engage with life from a place of conscious choice rather than reactive habit. This sense of freedom is seen as a fundamental step toward achieving the state of Clear, where the individual operates without the influence of past traumas.

Freedom from limitations on the Bridge isn't solely about eliminating negative experiences—it's also about unlocking **new abilities and insights**. Scientologists believe that each person has innate potential that lies dormant due to the suppressive effects of the reactive mind. As individuals move up the Bridge, they're encouraged to explore these latent abilities, which include heightened perception, improved communication skills, and increased resilience. This liberation enables Scientologists to function more effectively across all dynamics of existence, enhancing their personal lives, relationships, and contributions to society.

Achieving freedom on the Bridge also extends beyond the individual, as Scientologists believe that removing one's own limitations creates a positive ripple effect. For example, someone who has cleared their mind of reactive impulses can approach family, work, and group dynamics with more patience, empathy, and rationality. This approach not only benefits the individual but also those around them, as it fosters healthier, more constructive interactions. Scientologists see this as a way to support the broader goal of "Clearing the Planet," where each person's freedom contributes to a more ethical and harmonious world.

At the higher levels of the Bridge, particularly the **Operating Thetan (OT) levels**, the concept of freedom from limitations takes on a spiritual dimension. After reaching Clear, individuals begin to address deeper aspects of their existence as spiritual beings. These OT levels are thought to provide insights into the nature of life, the universe, and the spiritual self, further removing limitations that are not merely mental or emotional but transcend physical experience. Scientologists believe that these advanced levels help them reach a point where they're fully aware of their spiritual potential, achieving freedom on a much broader scale.

By moving up the Bridge, Scientologists aim to **remove the layers that cloud true understanding**. The goal is to experience life without the distortions introduced by fear, self-doubt, or unresolved trauma. Achieving freedom from these limitations means individuals can finally see themselves clearly, act with authenticity, and engage meaningfully with the world. Scientologists view this freedom as an essential part of their spiritual path, believing it brings them closer to true self-realization.

## The Role of Personal Responsibility on the Bridge

Personal responsibility is integral to the **Bridge to Total Freedom** in Scientology, as individuals are encouraged to take an active role in their own spiritual progress. The Bridge is not a passive journey; it requires conscious effort, dedication, and accountability at every level. Scientologists believe that progress on the Bridge is directly related to the willingness to address one's own limitations, confront past actions, and take responsibility for the impact of those actions. This commitment to personal responsibility is seen as essential for achieving the freedom and clarity offered by the Bridge.

The concept of **personal responsibility begins with auditing**. In each auditing session, individuals are expected to confront their own memories and experiences, taking ownership of the patterns that hold them back. Rather than blaming external factors or others for their issues, Scientologists are encouraged to look inward, examining how their choices and reactions have shaped their lives. This internal focus fosters a sense of agency, reinforcing the idea that each person has the power to change their circumstances by working through their own limitations.

Personal responsibility on the Bridge also involves **adhering to ethical standards** that support one's spiritual growth. Scientology emphasizes ethical conduct as a foundation for progress, with each level on the Bridge requiring individuals to align their actions with the principles of honesty, integrity, and accountability. Scientologists are encouraged to act in ways that promote survival and well-being for themselves, their families, groups, and society at large. By maintaining ethical responsibility, they believe they're creating a stable foundation for their spiritual journey, one that enables them to advance without self-imposed obstacles.

Taking responsibility on the Bridge extends to recognizing and addressing one's influence on others. Scientologists are taught that their actions affect those around them and that part of personal responsibility involves understanding these impacts. For example, an individual who has unresolved conflicts or unexamined behaviors may bring those issues into their relationships or group interactions, creating tension or misunderstanding. By actively working through the Bridge, they can address these influences, fostering healthier, more constructive interactions that benefit not only themselves but also those connected to them.

At the **Operating Thetan (OT) levels**, personal responsibility shifts to a higher plane, where individuals are encouraged to take responsibility for their own spiritual nature. At these advanced levels, responsibility becomes less about external actions and more about understanding the power and influence of the thetan. Scientologists believe that as they progress through the OT levels, they gain insight into their connection to the universe and their role within it. This expanded awareness requires them to take responsibility not only for their immediate actions but also for the broader implications of their existence as spiritual beings.

The emphasis on personal responsibility also reinforces the idea that **no one else can make progress for you** on the Bridge. Scientologists are taught that only they can address their reactive mind, confront engrams, and achieve Clear. This self-directed approach underscores the belief that spiritual freedom is earned through individual effort, not granted by an outside force. Personal responsibility is viewed as a guiding principle that affects every level of the Bridge, from the initial stages of mental clarity to the advanced stages of spiritual insight. Scientologists see it as the foundation of true freedom, as it encourages them to live deliberately, make ethical choices, and take control of their lives, fully capable of shaping their own future.

# CHAPTER 6: AUDITING - THE PATH TO SELF-DISCOVERY

## Definition and Purpose of Auditing

In Scientology, **auditing** is a central practice aimed at helping individuals achieve greater self-awareness, emotional freedom, and mental clarity. It's a structured form of spiritual counseling designed to guide people through past experiences, allowing them to address unresolved traumas and negative emotions. The ultimate purpose of auditing is to enable the person to confront and release the burdens of their past, paving the way for personal growth and self-discovery. Scientologists view auditing as a vital tool on their journey toward spiritual freedom, as it helps uncover and resolve the influences of the reactive mind.

Auditing sessions are one-on-one, with an **auditor** (a trained Scientologist) guiding the individual, known as the **preclear**. The auditor's role is not to judge or interpret but to provide support and ask specific questions that help the preclear recall and examine significant memories. The goal is to identify engrams—painful or traumatic memories stored in the reactive mind—that trigger irrational responses in daily life. By bringing these engrams to conscious awareness, the preclear can reprocess them, reducing their emotional impact and influence over behavior. This process is viewed as essential to moving toward the state of Clear, where the individual is free from the control of the reactive mind.

In auditing, **self-discovery** is achieved by diving into layers of memories and experiences that have accumulated over time. The practice emphasizes direct personal experience, allowing individuals to gain insight into their behaviors, fears, and limitations. As they progress, Scientologists believe that preclears become more attuned to their own thoughts and motivations, gaining clarity on what drives them and how past incidents have shaped their lives. This exploration helps them see patterns and connections that were previously hidden, enabling them to make conscious, rational choices rather than reacting unconsciously to old triggers.

A key part of the auditing process is the use of the **E-Meter**, a device that measures electrical resistance on the skin, indicating shifts in emotional response. Scientologists see the E-Meter as an aid to help locate areas of emotional charge. When the preclear speaks about a specific memory or experience, changes on the E-Meter can suggest the presence of an engram or unresolved issue. While the E-Meter doesn't analyze or "read" the mind, it provides the auditor with real-time feedback, which helps guide the session and focus on areas where the preclear may be holding onto emotional energy. For Scientologists, this tool is essential in making the auditing process efficient and effective.

Auditing sessions are structured around **specific commands or questions** aimed at uncovering particular types of memories or reactions. The auditor might ask the preclear to revisit a certain incident, encouraging them to recall the details and emotions associated with it. This revisiting allows the preclear to view the incident from a new perspective, often enabling them to release pent-up emotions or lingering fears. Scientologists believe that as these memories are reprocessed, they lose their power over the preclear's mind, gradually reducing the reactive mind's influence and enabling the analytical mind to take control.

The purpose of auditing goes beyond addressing individual memories; it's also about building **personal resilience and mental clarity**. As preclears confront and release old traumas, they develop a greater capacity to handle life's challenges with confidence and stability. Auditing is intended to equip individuals with the mental tools needed to face adversity without reverting to automatic, emotional responses rooted in past pain. Scientologists see this as an important step toward achieving independence and self-determination, where the individual is no longer held back by unprocessed experiences.

Auditing sessions are conducted with a strict code of **confidentiality and ethics**. Scientologists believe that maintaining a safe, respectful environment is essential for effective auditing, as it allows the preclear to explore deeply personal and potentially painful memories without fear of judgment or disclosure. The auditor follows a set of standards to ensure that the session remains focused on the preclear's needs and progression. This ethical commitment is seen as central to the auditing process, reinforcing trust between the auditor and preclear.

As a practice, auditing is designed to be cumulative, with each session building upon the last. Scientologists believe that as individuals go through multiple sessions, they progressively free themselves from engrams, achieving **incremental gains in awareness and clarity**. Each step taken in auditing is seen as part of the larger journey on the Bridge to Total Freedom, where the person is working toward a state of Clear and, eventually, higher levels of spiritual awareness. For Scientologists, auditing is not just a therapeutic tool; it's a disciplined, ongoing process aimed at realizing the full potential of the self, addressing mental and emotional barriers that hinder true spiritual growth.

## The Role of the E-Meter in Auditing

In auditing, the **E-Meter** (or electropsychometer) serves as a key tool to help individuals identify and process mental and emotional barriers. Scientologists view the E-Meter as an instrument that assists in locating engrams, or stored memories of past pain and trauma, which are believed to impact the preclear's behavior and responses. The device is designed to detect changes in electrical resistance on the skin when a person recalls certain thoughts or memories, indicating areas that may carry an emotional charge. Although the E-Meter doesn't analyze or interpret, Scientologists believe it provides helpful feedback for the auditing process by highlighting moments of emotional significance.

The E-Meter consists of a small electronic device connected to two metal cans, which the preclear holds in each hand during the session. When the preclear begins discussing a specific topic, memory, or question, the E-Meter measures the electrical response on the skin, shown as needle movements on the device's display. These needle movements, according to Scientologists, can signal the presence of engrams or unresolved issues. When the needle reacts strongly, it may suggest that the preclear has encountered a significant mental barrier or memory with lingering emotional weight. This feedback helps the auditor guide the session, focusing on areas that appear to hold the most relevance.

For the auditor, the E-Meter acts as a **non-verbal indicator** of the preclear's inner responses, which might not be immediately apparent through verbal communication alone. The auditor uses the E-Meter's readings to refine questions and help the preclear examine experiences in greater depth. For example, if a particular question or topic causes the needle to react noticeably, the auditor might continue to explore that line of inquiry, encouraging the preclear to confront and address any associated thoughts or emotions. This process, Scientologists believe, enables more efficient identification and resolution of mental blocks.

The E-Meter is also used to **track progress** throughout the auditing session. As the preclear discusses a particular memory or issue, the initial needle reaction may lessen or stabilize as the session continues. Scientologists interpret this change as a sign that the preclear is successfully confronting and releasing the emotional charge tied to the engram. Over time, the preclear may reach a point where discussing the memory no longer causes significant needle movement, which is seen as an indication that the issue has been addressed and cleared.

Scientologists view the E-Meter as an essential component of the **self-discovery process** in auditing. By providing real-time feedback, it allows preclears to gain insights into hidden aspects of their minds, helping them see where unresolved issues might be influencing their thoughts and actions. Although the device itself doesn't "solve" problems, it aids in guiding the session toward areas that can benefit from conscious examination. For Scientologists, this focused exploration through the E-Meter contributes significantly to achieving a state of greater mental clarity and emotional freedom.

## Processes and Techniques in Auditing

In auditing, **specific processes and techniques** are employed to help individuals identify and confront engrams—memories of past pain and trauma—so they can experience greater freedom and clarity. Auditing sessions are structured around a series of commands or questions designed to guide the preclear through their memories and mental landscape. These processes help the preclear examine areas of their life where unresolved issues may linger, enabling them to process and release these experiences.

One of the core techniques in auditing is called **recall processing**. In this technique, the auditor asks the preclear to remember and describe a past experience in as much detail as possible. The auditor may repeat the command or question to encourage the preclear to continue exploring the memory. By revisiting specific incidents, the preclear confronts the emotions, physical sensations, and thoughts tied to the memory. Scientologists believe that by examining these memories without suppression or avoidance, the preclear can reduce the emotional charge they hold, thereby weakening the grip of the reactive mind.

Another common technique used in auditing is **confront processing**, which involves having the preclear face certain thoughts or feelings directly, without judgment or analysis. The auditor may ask the preclear to simply acknowledge and observe specific sensations or memories. Confront processing is intended to help the preclear become comfortable with emotions or thoughts they may have previously avoided. This practice is viewed as essential for building resilience, as it allows the preclear to face potentially distressing memories without feeling overwhelmed or controlled by them.

**Repetitive processes** are also used in auditing, where the same question or command is repeated multiple times within a session. This repetition is meant to encourage the preclear to explore different aspects of a single experience, gradually revealing deeper insights and reducing the engram's emotional charge. Scientologists believe that through this method, the preclear gains a clearer understanding of how the reactive mind operates and is able to address lingering mental barriers. By working through repetitive processes, the preclear can gradually eliminate automatic responses that were previously dictated by past trauma.

Another key technique is **the Precept Process**, where the auditor asks the preclear to consider hypothetical scenarios or alternative perspectives related to a past experience. This technique is used to encourage the preclear to see their memories from a new angle, allowing for cognitive shifts and re-evaluation. For example, the auditor might ask the preclear to imagine handling a similar situation differently or to examine how their response could have impacted others. This broader perspective helps the preclear understand their actions and reactions more fully, encouraging more conscious decision-making in future situations.

These techniques work together to create a structured approach to **self-discovery and emotional release**. Scientologists believe that auditing's guided processes allow individuals to confront and understand their experiences, gradually dissolving the reactive mind's influence. Each technique is tailored to uncover and process engrams, enabling the preclear to experience life with greater clarity and control.

# The Importance of Auditor-Preclear Relationship

In auditing, the **relationship between the auditor and preclear** is vital to the effectiveness of the process. This relationship is based on trust, respect, and a shared commitment to achieving mental clarity and personal growth. Scientologists believe that the auditor-preclear dynamic greatly influences the success of auditing sessions, as it creates a safe and supportive environment where the preclear feels comfortable exploring sensitive or difficult memories. A strong relationship encourages open communication and helps the preclear feel understood and guided.

The auditor's primary role is to **guide without interpreting**. In Scientology, auditors are trained to avoid offering opinions, judgments, or personal interpretations of the preclear's experiences. This approach allows the preclear to process their own memories without external influence, which Scientologists believe is essential for true self-discovery. By remaining neutral and objective, the auditor enables the preclear to reach their own insights, creating an environment where the preclear can safely confront engrams and emotional challenges. This neutrality helps build trust, as the preclear knows they can speak freely without fear of criticism or interference.

**Confidentiality is strictly upheld** in the auditor-preclear relationship. Scientology places a high value on privacy within auditing sessions, believing that confidentiality is critical to fostering trust. Knowing that their disclosures will remain private allows the preclear to go into personal and sometimes painful memories without reservation. This commitment to confidentiality is seen as a fundamental part of the auditor's role, reinforcing the safe space needed for effective auditing. For the preclear, the assurance of privacy supports a more open and honest exploration of their past.

**Empathy and patience** are also important qualities in an auditor, as auditing can be an intense and emotionally charged experience. The auditor's role is to support the preclear as they revisit difficult memories and process strong emotions. Through active listening and gentle guidance, the auditor helps the preclear feel grounded and focused. This emotional support is seen as necessary for navigating the often challenging path of self-discovery, as it enables the preclear to engage fully with their experiences without feeling overwhelmed. Scientologists believe that an empathetic auditor creates a sense of partnership, where both are working toward the common goal of mental and spiritual freedom.

The auditor-preclear relationship is based on **clear communication and consistency**. Auditors follow specific procedures and ask questions in a structured manner to maintain the focus and flow of each session. This consistency helps the preclear stay engaged with the process, as the auditing sessions have a predictable rhythm and purpose. By maintaining a structured approach, the auditor ensures that the preclear's journey is gradual and steady, building trust in the process and reinforcing the preclear's commitment to self-discovery. Scientologists believe that this systematic communication style helps the preclear feel supported and guided throughout their journey on the Bridge.

The **non-judgmental, supportive approach** taken by the auditor is seen as essential for effective auditing. The preclear is encouraged to look deeply into their own thoughts and memories, free from outside influence. Scientologists believe that this relationship enables individuals to access insights that might otherwise remain hidden. Through patient guidance, confidentiality, and emotional support, the auditor helps the preclear confront and release the limitations that have shaped their lives.

# CHAPTER 7: THE STATE OF CLEAR

## The Characteristics of a Clear Mind

In Scientology, a **Clear mind** represents a state of freedom from the reactive mind, where a person is no longer controlled by past traumas, irrational fears, or automatic responses rooted in painful memories. The mind of someone who has reached Clear is considered stable, focused, and resilient. This level of clarity allows them to navigate life with a sense of control, engaging fully with each moment without interference from past negative experiences.

One of the primary characteristics of a Clear mind is its **ability to function without engrams**. Engrams are stored memories of past painful or traumatic events that remain in the reactive mind, often influencing behavior unconsciously. In a Clear, these engrams are no longer present, meaning that the mind operates without emotional charge from past traumas. Without engrams, a person is free to think and act based on present circumstances rather than past triggers. This results in a more rational and deliberate approach to challenges, allowing Clears to respond calmly and effectively.

A Clear mind is also **marked by heightened self-awareness**. In Scientology, this means a person understands their own thoughts, feelings, and motivations clearly, without confusion or ambiguity. Clears are seen as capable of examining their actions and decisions with objectivity, able to make choices that align with their true goals and values. This self-awareness is essential for personal growth, as it enables Clears to identify their strengths and address areas where they want to improve. The absence of the reactive mind's influence allows them to explore their thoughts and behaviors without fear of uncovering painful or unwanted memories.

**Emotional stability** is another defining feature of a Clear mind. Without the automatic responses tied to the reactive mind, Clears are less likely to be thrown off balance by unexpected events or stressors. Their emotional responses are considered more measured and proportionate, allowing them to handle difficulties without becoming overwhelmed. For example, in a challenging situation, a Clear might feel a range of emotions but remains centered and able to assess the situation logically. Scientologists believe that this emotional steadiness contributes to a sense of inner peace and resilience, enabling Clears to face life with confidence and composure.

In addition to emotional stability, a Clear mind is **marked by greater intellectual clarity**. With the reactive mind no longer influencing thoughts, Clears can concentrate more effectively and process information with greater accuracy. They are believed to experience improved memory, enhanced problem-solving skills, and a sharper focus on goals. Scientologists see this intellectual clarity as a natural result of clearing the mind of irrational influences, allowing the individual's analytical mind to function optimally. This enhanced mental acuity supports success across personal, professional, and social domains, as Clears can engage more fully with tasks and challenges.

A Clear mind also demonstrates **heightened ethical awareness**. Scientologists believe that without the distortions caused by engrams, Clears are better equipped to act in alignment with their principles and values. This ethical awareness is thought to come from a place of genuine understanding rather than reactive behavior. Clears are believed to naturally make choices that reflect integrity, honesty, and respect for others, as their actions are no longer shaped by unconscious fears or unresolved conflicts. This ethical clarity is seen as essential for maintaining healthy relationships and contributing positively to groups, as it promotes trust and accountability.

Clears experience **an increased sense of personal responsibility** as well. With the reactive mind cleared, individuals no longer feel compelled to blame others or circumstances for their struggles or challenges. Instead, they accept responsibility for their actions and outcomes, understanding that they have the power to shape their lives consciously. This self-directed approach is fundamental to the state of Clear, as it reinforces the idea that true freedom comes from owning one's choices and taking control of one's destiny. Scientologists believe that this personal accountability enables Clears to live authentically and make decisions that contribute to their long-term well-being.

Finally, **freedom from irrational fears and anxieties** is a key characteristic of a Clear mind. Scientologists believe that many fears stem from past traumas stored in the reactive mind, which create automatic responses of fear or avoidance. In the state of Clear, these reactions are no longer present, allowing individuals to face situations without undue apprehension. This freedom from fear opens up new possibilities for personal growth, as Clears are more willing to take on challenges, explore new experiences, and interact openly with others.

In essence, a Clear mind is described as free, focused, and fully conscious. Scientologists view it as a state of profound mental and emotional liberation, where the individual can live purposefully, connect authentically with others, and experience life without the shadow of past pain or limitation.

## Emotional and Spiritual Benefits of Being Clear

In the state of Clear, individuals experience a profound shift in their emotional and spiritual well-being. Without the influence of engrams and the reactive mind, Clears can navigate life with greater emotional stability and inner peace. **One of the primary emotional benefits** of being Clear is freedom from irrational fears, anxieties, and automatic responses. Since engrams—painful memories stored in the reactive mind—are no longer present, Clears don't face the emotional triggers that once influenced their actions and reactions. This means they can respond to situations based on current circumstances rather than past trauma, allowing them to engage with life in a balanced, calm way.

Clears also experience a deeper **sense of happiness and contentment**. Scientologists believe that by removing the burdens of past pain, individuals are free to enjoy life without the weight of unresolved issues. This emotional freedom contributes to a more positive outlook and an enhanced ability to experience joy. Clears are less affected by minor stresses and daily irritations, as they have released the stored emotional charge tied to their past. This openness allows them to connect more deeply with others, enjoy their relationships, and feel genuine satisfaction in everyday interactions.

The spiritual benefits of being Clear are equally significant. Scientologists hold that the reactive mind's influence limits spiritual awareness, creating a fog that blocks true self-understanding. In the state of Clear, this fog lifts, revealing the thetan's true nature. Clears gain an **enhanced sense of spiritual identity**, with a clearer understanding of their purpose and existence. This heightened awareness enables them to connect more deeply with the Eight Dynamics, particularly the spiritual aspects of life. They experience a stronger connection to their inner self, enabling them to pursue their spiritual journey with greater focus and clarity.

Clears are believed to achieve **a sense of unity with others and the universe**, viewing life as interconnected and meaningful. With the reactive mind's barriers removed, they feel more aligned with the spiritual dimensions of existence, fostering a sense of compassion and respect for life. This spiritual clarity is thought to make Clears more receptive to advanced stages of awareness, as they're no longer hindered by unresolved traumas or automatic defenses. For Scientologists, this state of spiritual harmony is essential for moving forward on the Bridge to Total Freedom, as it establishes a foundation of inner peace and connection.

By reaching Clear, individuals also gain an **increased capacity for ethical behavior**. The absence of the reactive mind's influence allows them to make decisions based on reason, empathy, and ethical considerations rather than irrational impulses. This freedom supports a more genuine alignment with one's values, allowing Clears to act with integrity and purpose. Scientologists believe that this alignment not only benefits the individual but also enhances their relationships and contributions to the community, as Clears interact with others in a more honest and respectful manner.

## Personal Transformation and Self-Realization

In Scientology, achieving the state of Clear is seen as a powerful catalyst for **personal transformation and self-realization**. Without the reactive mind's influence, individuals undergo a transformation in how they perceive themselves, interact with others, and engage with the world. Scientologists view this transformation as a natural outcome of addressing the deep-seated issues and traumas stored in the reactive mind. Once these mental and emotional blocks are removed, Clears can experience life from a new perspective, grounded in self-awareness and clarity.

**A critical aspect of this transformation** is the release of automatic responses tied to engrams. Before reaching Clear, individuals may find themselves reacting impulsively, driven by memories of past pain that resurface in everyday situations. In the state of Clear, these engrams no longer dictate behavior. The result is a greater sense of control and self-determination, allowing individuals to make conscious choices based on present realities rather than past fears or traumas. This level of personal autonomy enables Clears to approach life with confidence, free from the emotional baggage that once influenced their actions.

The journey to Clear also brings about a **heightened sense of self-awareness**. Without the distortions caused by the reactive mind, individuals gain a clearer understanding of their motivations, desires, and goals. They can examine their own thoughts and actions with objectivity, making it easier to identify areas for growth or improvement. Scientologists believe that this level of self-awareness is essential for personal development, as it encourages individuals to live in alignment with their true values and aspirations. This self-reflection allows Clears to build meaningful relationships, set and achieve goals, and contribute positively to the community.

Self-realization in the state of Clear also involves **rediscovering the thetan's true nature**. In Scientology, the thetan is the spiritual self, which is often obscured by the reactive mind's automatic responses and unresolved issues. By clearing these barriers, individuals gain a direct connection to their spiritual identity, allowing them to understand themselves as thetans rather than just physical beings. This recognition fosters a deeper sense of purpose, as Clears come to view their life as part of a larger spiritual journey. Scientologists see this self-realization as essential for advancing further on the Bridge, where they will explore increasingly profound aspects of their spiritual identity.

Through personal transformation, Clears experience a **renewed sense of responsibility and ethical clarity**. Freed from the reactive mind's influence, they can act in ways that align with their values and principles. This ethical alignment enables them to make decisions that benefit themselves and others, enhancing the quality of their relationships and contributions to the community. Scientologists believe that Clears are better equipped to take on roles of responsibility, as their actions are guided by rational thought and ethical understanding rather than automatic, reactive behavior.

Finally, personal transformation at the state of Clear enhances **emotional resilience and adaptability**. With past traumas resolved, Clears are better prepared to face new challenges, handle stress, and adapt to changes without losing balance. This resilience enables them to engage fully with life's experiences, exploring new possibilities and setting higher aspirations. In this way, self-realization in the state of Clear is not static; it is an ongoing process where individuals continue to grow, learn, and evolve in alignment with their true potential.

## Reaching a Stable State of Awareness

In the state of Clear, individuals achieve a **stable state of awareness** that allows them to engage with life fully and without the interruptions of the reactive mind. This stability is one of the defining aspects of being Clear, as it represents a consistent, balanced state in which the individual is unaffected by automatic responses or irrational fears. Scientologists believe that this stable awareness is essential for living a conscious, intentional life, as it enables individuals to make clear-headed decisions and respond to situations based on logic and understanding.

A key characteristic of this stable awareness is **freedom from emotional reactivity**. In the reactive mind, memories of past pain or trauma can trigger automatic responses, such as fear, anger, or avoidance. These reactions disrupt a person's awareness and create emotional turbulence. In the state of Clear, these automatic responses are no longer present, allowing the individual to remain calm and composed even in challenging situations. This freedom from reactivity contributes to a steady emotional foundation, enabling Clears to handle stress and adversity with confidence and rationality.

With a stable state of awareness, Clears experience an **enhanced ability to stay present**. Scientologists believe that many people are unconsciously influenced by past experiences, which can draw them away from the current moment. In the state of Clear, however, individuals are no longer burdened by unresolved memories or emotional residues from the past. This clarity allows them to focus fully on the present, engaging deeply with their surroundings and relationships. For Clears, this present-focused awareness supports greater mindfulness, concentration, and effectiveness in daily life.

This stability also extends to **ethical and moral clarity**. Without the influence of the reactive mind, Clears are believed to have a stronger understanding of right and wrong, guided by their true values rather than unconscious fears or biases. This ethical clarity enables them to act with integrity, fostering trust and respect in their relationships. Scientologists see this as a core benefit of reaching Clear, as it promotes genuine, honest interactions with others and aligns the individual's actions with their principles.

A stable state of awareness in the Clear mind includes **improved problem-solving abilities**. With the analytical mind unobstructed by reactive responses, Clears can approach challenges with clarity and precision. This enhanced mental acuity allows them to assess situations logically, consider multiple perspectives, and make informed decisions. Scientologists believe that this mental sharpness supports both personal and professional success, as it enables individuals to engage with complex issues thoughtfully and confidently. This approach encourages Clears to set and achieve goals, address obstacles effectively, and adapt to new situations with ease.

Lastly, a Clear's stable awareness fosters a **strong sense of inner peace and self-assurance**. Without the interference of unresolved emotions or reactive impulses, Clears feel more comfortable with themselves and their place in the world. This inner stability creates a foundation for self-confidence, as Clears no longer experience the inner conflicts or self-doubts that once hindered them. Scientologists view this peace as a critical part of achieving a fulfilled life, as it allows Clears to explore new experiences, build meaningful connections, and pursue higher levels of spiritual awareness on the Bridge to Total Freedom.

# CHAPTER 8: THE OPERATING THETAN (OT) LEVELS

## Overview of OT Levels and Spiritual Powers

The **Operating Thetan (OT) Levels** in Scientology represent advanced stages on the Bridge to Total Freedom, focusing on a person's abilities as a spiritual being, or thetan. These levels are designed to expand awareness beyond the physical world, unlocking spiritual powers and insights that Scientologists believe are inherent to each thetan. While earlier steps on the Bridge focus on clearing the reactive mind and achieving mental clarity, the OT levels guide individuals toward understanding and enhancing their spiritual capacities, moving closer to a state of total freedom.

The word **"Operating"** in Operating Thetan signifies that the thetan is functioning independently of the mind and body, capable of influencing life and the universe at a higher level. At the OT levels, Scientologists believe they can achieve greater awareness of their spiritual identity and explore the true nature of the universe. Each OT level is structured to build on the insights and progress gained in the previous levels, gradually guiding individuals to experience their spiritual abilities and powers firsthand.

**OT I**, the introductory OT level, is often focused on enhancing self-awareness. Scientologists at OT I start with exercises that help them identify their spiritual presence and learn to differentiate it from the mind and body. This level is intended to make the person more aware of themselves as a thetan, recognizing the influence they have over their thoughts, actions, and surroundings. OT I is seen as a foundation for the deeper spiritual exploration that follows, setting the stage for expanding awareness beyond personal experiences.

Moving into **OT II**, Scientologists confront barriers that limit spiritual freedom. OT II involves processes that are intended to eliminate fixed ideas, mental patterns, or negative influences that restrict spiritual awareness. By addressing these limitations, OT II aims to increase the thetan's ability to perceive reality clearly, without interference from past conditioning. This level is thought to deepen an individual's understanding of their spiritual nature, freeing them from limitations that may have accumulated over countless lifetimes.

At **OT III**, known as the "Wall of Fire," Scientologists encounter more challenging processes intended to help them overcome significant barriers to spiritual freedom. OT III is described as a breakthrough point where individuals confront deep-seated issues that go beyond personal traumas, addressing what Scientologists believe are universal barriers affecting all thetans. The purpose of OT III is to reach a level of self-mastery and resilience that enables the thetan to operate with greater freedom. It's at this level that Scientologists often report profound insights into the spiritual world, gaining a new perspective on their role in the universe.

**OT IV through OT VII** continue this journey, each level introducing increasingly complex exercises aimed at enhancing the thetan's abilities. **OT IV** is known as the "Clearing Course," where individuals focus on removing additional obstacles that could cloud spiritual perception. At **OT V and OT VI**, Scientologists are taught techniques that are believed to enable them to take greater control over their mental and physical environment. These levels emphasize gaining a more refined understanding of spiritual powers, allowing the thetan to extend its influence beyond the self.

**OT VII**, often referred to as "Cause Over Life," focuses on the thetan's power to influence life. Scientologists working on OT VII engage in practices aimed at heightening their perception, with the goal of being able to direct their spiritual energy more effectively. This level is designed to give the individual a sense of mastery over their life, fostering a sense of control and purpose that transcends everyday experiences. By reaching OT VII, Scientologists believe they've gained the ability to shape their reality in alignment with their spiritual goals.

The final level currently available, **OT VIII**, is known as "Truth Revealed." This level is intended to bring about a state of full spiritual awareness and understanding of the universe and existence. Scientologists who reach OT VIII are considered to have achieved a high degree of insight, seeing reality from a perspective that is unhindered by mental or physical limitations. OT VIII is seen as the pinnacle of the OT levels, where individuals attain what Scientologists describe as a state of spiritual freedom and enlightenment.

Each OT level is structured with specific exercises, known as **processes**, designed to enhance spiritual awareness and thetan abilities. These processes range from guided self-reflection to complex techniques intended to confront and resolve spiritual barriers. Scientologists believe that as they progress through these levels, they gradually reclaim spiritual powers that may have been lost or obscured over time. These powers are not physical or supernatural but are seen as inherent capacities of the thetan, such as heightened perception, the ability to direct thoughts, and greater influence over their surroundings.

The journey through the OT levels is deeply personal, and Scientologists view each level as a stepping stone toward full self-realization. By working through the challenges and insights offered at each OT level, Scientologists believe they come to understand themselves as spiritual beings, with powers and purposes that extend beyond the physical realm.

## Goals and Practices of Operating Thetan Levels

The **Operating Thetan (OT) levels** in Scientology are designed to guide individuals on a journey of spiritual awakening and empowerment. Each OT level has specific goals and practices, aimed at enhancing the thetan's abilities and awareness. The primary goal across all OT levels is to enable the thetan to operate independently of the mind and body, gradually uncovering the true potential of one's spiritual essence. Scientologists view these levels as a structured path to reclaiming spiritual abilities that are considered dormant or obscured by mental barriers.

At **OT I**, the initial goal is to increase self-awareness. Practices at this level include exercises that focus on observing one's own spiritual presence and learning to identify oneself as a thetan, distinct from the mind and body. These practices lay the groundwork for a deeper understanding of the spiritual self, creating a foundation for further exploration. Through these exercises, individuals begin to develop a heightened sense of spiritual presence and purpose.

As individuals progress to **OT II**, the goals shift toward identifying and erasing fixed ideas and mental patterns that limit spiritual freedom. The practices at OT II include specific processes aimed at clearing mental constructs and conditioning accumulated over lifetimes. Scientologists believe these practices help eliminate influences that cloud spiritual perception, allowing the thetan to function with greater clarity and autonomy. By addressing these fixed patterns, Scientologists aim to remove subconscious obstacles that restrict their spiritual awareness.

**OT III**, also known as the "Wall of Fire," represents a pivotal stage in the OT journey. The goal here is to confront and overcome fundamental barriers to spiritual freedom that are believed to impact all thetans. The practices at this level are more intensive and involve addressing significant spiritual challenges. OT III processes are designed to increase resilience and self-mastery, helping individuals gain a profound understanding of their spiritual existence. By completing OT III, Scientologists believe they've broken through major limitations that once restricted their spiritual potential.

At **OT IV through OT VI**, the goals focus on refining spiritual powers and expanding influence. OT IV, often called the "Clearing Course," involves clearing out any lingering barriers that may prevent full spiritual perception. OT V and OT VI include techniques that allow Scientologists to exert greater control over their mental and physical environment, cultivating abilities that extend beyond the self. The practices here emphasize strengthening the connection between the thetan and their surrounding reality, encouraging a more refined sense of spiritual direction and power.

The goal at **OT VII**, known as "Cause Over Life," is to achieve mastery over life experiences. Practices at this level involve enhancing perception and directing spiritual energy in alignment with one's intentions. Scientologists believe that the exercises at OT VII help individuals achieve a sense of control and purpose, enabling them to influence their reality effectively. This level is often viewed as the culmination of significant spiritual empowerment, as the thetan becomes increasingly capable of shaping their life according to their goals and values.

The ultimate goal of **OT VIII**, the highest level currently available, is full spiritual awareness and insight into the universe's truths. OT VIII practices are believed to reveal profound understandings of existence, allowing individuals to see reality unfiltered by physical or mental constraints. Scientologists who reach OT VIII are considered to have achieved a high level of spiritual freedom and mastery, completing the path laid out by the OT levels. This mastery is seen as an alignment with universal truths, enabling the individual to fully realize their potential as a thetan.

## The Path to OT VIII and Spiritual Mastery

The **path to OT VIII** is an incremental journey designed to guide Scientologists toward what they see as ultimate spiritual mastery. Each OT level serves as a step that builds upon the insights and skills gained in previous stages, gradually leading to a more profound understanding of one's spiritual identity and potential. For Scientologists, reaching OT VIII is considered the culmination of a lifelong pursuit of self-discovery, where the individual attains a high degree of awareness and independence from the limitations of the physical world.

As Scientologists progress through **OT I to OT VII**, each level helps them confront increasingly complex aspects of their spiritual self. At OT I, individuals begin with exercises focused on increasing self-awareness and recognizing their spiritual essence. This early stage allows them to distinguish their true identity as a thetan, laying the groundwork for more advanced spiritual work. The journey then continues through OT II and OT III, where individuals confront deeper layers of mental patterns and barriers. OT III, often called the "Wall of Fire," is seen as a significant breakthrough point, as it involves facing universal challenges that are believed to affect all thetans.

OT IV through OT VI focus on enhancing spiritual powers and influence. **OT IV**, known as the "Clearing Course," is intended to clear out residual barriers that may cloud perception or restrict spiritual growth. At OT V and OT VI, Scientologists work on processes that are said to grant them greater control over their mental and physical surroundings, increasing their ability to act intentionally as spiritual beings. The practices in these levels emphasize achieving more refined skills, aligning the thetan's purpose with their environment.

**OT VII**, or "Cause Over Life," represents a crucial phase before OT VIII. Here, Scientologists work to heighten their awareness and strengthen their ability to influence life events. This level focuses on enhancing the thetan's power to shape experiences according to their spiritual goals. The intention is for individuals to gain a strong sense of purpose and mastery over their existence, preparing them for the profound insights awaiting them at OT VIII.

**OT VIII**, titled "Truth Revealed," is seen as the pinnacle of the OT journey. Scientologists view OT VIII as the level where they achieve full spiritual mastery, understanding the fundamental truths of existence. The path to OT VIII is challenging, requiring dedication and an increasing sense of personal responsibility at each level. The journey to OT VIII allows Scientologists to transcend their previous limitations, ultimately reaching a state of enlightenment and spiritual freedom. Scientologists believe that at OT VIII, they achieve a clear and unobstructed view of the universe and their place within it, unburdened by mental or physical restraints.

This path toward OT VIII isn't solely about personal gain but about aligning with the greater purposes of life and the universe. Scientologists believe that each OT level refines their ability to act in harmony with the Eight Dynamics, creating an interconnected relationship between self-improvement and the well-being of all existence. The path to OT VIII is one of transformation, where individuals evolve from managing personal challenges to attaining a higher awareness that connects them to a broader spiritual understanding.

## OT Levels as Paths to Higher Awareness

The **OT levels** in Scientology are structured as pathways to reach higher levels of spiritual awareness, guiding individuals through stages of self-discovery and awakening. Each OT level represents a step toward expanding the thetan's perception and abilities, moving beyond mental clarity to spiritual insight. Scientologists see the OT levels as a gradual progression that allows them to understand life from a broader perspective, enhancing their awareness of themselves, others, and the universe.

Starting with **OT I**, the journey begins with developing heightened self-awareness. At this introductory level, individuals engage in exercises designed to help them recognize themselves as spiritual beings distinct from their minds and bodies. This initial step is seen as foundational, creating an awareness of one's spiritual presence and purpose. The heightened self-recognition achieved at OT I prepares individuals for the more intensive exploration that follows in the subsequent levels.

At **OT II**, the focus shifts to clearing mental patterns and fixed ideas that limit spiritual perception. The practices at this level are aimed at removing mental conditioning and subconscious patterns that block awareness. By addressing these influences, Scientologists believe they can perceive reality with greater clarity, free from preconceived notions. This level encourages individuals to let go of past constraints, opening them up to a clearer and more expansive view of themselves and the world.

OT III, known as the "Wall of Fire," is where Scientologists confront significant spiritual barriers. This level is thought to reveal deep-seated issues that impact all thetans, presenting challenges that require inner strength and resilience. Scientologists view OT III as a pivotal step that enables them to face obstacles they might not even be consciously aware of. By overcoming these barriers, they aim to gain a broader awareness that transcends the personal and connects them with universal truths.

**OT IV through OT VI** continue to build on this expanded awareness, refining the thetan's abilities to perceive and influence their environment. OT IV, the "Clearing Course," is intended to eliminate any remaining limitations, while OT V and OT VI focus on developing greater control over one's surroundings. These levels enhance the individual's capacity to interact with the world from a spiritual standpoint, allowing them to experience life with heightened awareness and influence.

At **OT VII**, called "Cause Over Life," the focus shifts to achieving a deeper mastery over life itself. This level involves processes that further sharpen the thetan's perception, enabling them to act with purpose and clarity. OT VII emphasizes aligning one's spiritual power with personal intentions, fostering a state of awareness that encompasses all aspects of existence. This level is seen as a profound step toward understanding one's purpose, as Scientologists believe that the thetan can now act with deliberate awareness and intention.

**OT VIII**, the final level currently available, is known as "Truth Revealed." Scientologists consider OT VIII the culmination of the journey toward higher awareness, where individuals attain a state of spiritual enlightenment. At this level, they are believed to experience reality without distortion, achieving a profound understanding of existence and their place within it. OT VIII represents a heightened level of awareness that aligns the thetan with the fundamental truths of the universe, creating a sense of spiritual harmony that is both powerful and peaceful.

The OT levels are seen as transformative paths that gradually lead to greater awareness and self-realization. By moving through these stages, Scientologists believe they can unlock deeper layers of perception, allowing them to experience life from a perspective that goes beyond physical and mental limitations.

# CHAPTER 9: THE ROLE OF TRAINING AND COURSES

## Scientology Academies and Levels of Training

In Scientology, **academies and training levels** are designed to provide members with structured education in the principles, practices, and skills essential to their spiritual journey. Scientology academies serve as centers of learning where members can engage deeply with the teachings of L. Ron Hubbard, gaining practical skills that support their progress on the Bridge to Total Freedom. These academies offer various courses tailored to meet the needs of individuals at different stages of understanding, from beginners seeking foundational knowledge to advanced students preparing for higher responsibilities.

Each academy is organized to provide a **step-by-step training path** that allows Scientologists to learn and apply the concepts of auditing, communication, and personal development. Training at these levels isn't solely about acquiring theoretical knowledge; it emphasizes hands-on learning and practical application. Courses often include lectures, exercises, and written materials that are studied in a self-paced environment, allowing each student to master the material before advancing. This personalized approach ensures that students fully understand and integrate the teachings before moving to more complex topics.

Training at Scientology academies starts with **introductory courses** designed for those new to Scientology's principles. Courses like the Communication Course and the Success Through Communication Course teach fundamental skills, such as how to communicate effectively, listen actively, and handle misunderstandings. These courses introduce essential tools that students will use throughout their training, establishing a strong foundation in the basics of communication and interaction. By learning these skills early on, students build confidence in their ability to apply Scientology's principles in their daily lives, enhancing their relationships and interactions.

As students advance, they move to **intermediate levels of training**, where they learn more about auditing, the Bridge, and their role as potential auditors. At this stage, students take courses that cover the theory and methods behind auditing, such as the Hubbard Professional Auditor Course. This course goes into the mechanics of auditing, teaching students how to guide others through the auditing process while remaining neutral and supportive. Training at this level includes both theoretical study and practical exercises, where students practice the techniques they've learned in a supervised setting. This structured approach allows them to refine their skills under guidance, ensuring they're prepared to assist others effectively.

For those who wish to become professional auditors, **advanced levels of training** are available. Courses like the Class IV Auditor Course and the Academy Levels (Levels 0 to IV) prepare students to audit others across a range of auditing levels. These courses are intensive and require a deep commitment to mastering auditing skills. At the Academy Levels, each course focuses on a specific set of auditing skills, progressively building a comprehensive understanding of auditing theory and practice. By completing these levels, students are certified to deliver auditing to other Scientologists, assisting them in progressing on the Bridge. This advanced training enables auditors to work with a wide range of individuals, helping others achieve greater mental clarity and spiritual awareness.

Beyond individual courses, **Scientology academies foster an environment of ongoing learning and self-improvement**. Students are encouraged to continually refine their skills, review earlier materials, and seek deeper understanding of core concepts. This commitment to continuous education is central to Scientology's approach to training. Even experienced auditors return to academies to review techniques, learn new approaches, and stay updated with the latest developments in auditing and Scientology practices. This culture of lifelong learning ensures that Scientologists are consistently improving their understanding and ability to apply Hubbard's teachings.

Each level of training has **specific objectives and measurable outcomes**, which allows students to track their progress as they advance through the courses. Upon completing a course, students demonstrate their understanding and proficiency, often through practical application or supervised exercises. The goal is for students to leave each level with the confidence and competence to use their skills effectively. In addition, the structured training ensures that students gain a well-rounded education in Scientology, preparing them to take on greater responsibilities within the Church if they choose to pursue advanced roles.

Training in Scientology academies also emphasizes **the importance of ethics and integrity** in auditing and spiritual practice. Ethical training is integrated into many courses, particularly those focused on auditing. Scientologists are taught that ethical conduct is foundational to the success of any auditing session, as it fosters trust and creates a safe environment for self-discovery. Auditors are trained to uphold confidentiality, remain non-judgmental, and handle sensitive information responsibly. By embedding these ethical principles into training, Scientology ensures that its auditors maintain high standards of integrity, ultimately benefiting both the auditor and the preclear.

Scientology academies are dedicated to helping members develop both spiritually and practically, guiding them through each stage of their personal journey with the support and resources they need. Through this structured, supportive training environment, Scientologists learn the skills to navigate their spiritual path effectively and, if they choose, to help others do the same.

# Key Courses: Understanding Self and Others

In Scientology, training courses are structured to help individuals deepen their understanding of themselves and improve their relationships with others. These **key courses** provide foundational skills in communication, self-awareness, and interpersonal dynamics. One of the most widely attended courses is the **Success Through Communication Course**, which focuses on effective communication techniques. This course teaches participants how to listen actively, respond appropriately, and manage conversations constructively. Through drills and exercises, students learn to communicate with clarity and confidence, a skill Scientologists view as essential for both personal growth and social harmony.

The **Personal Values and Integrity Course** is another significant course, focusing on helping individuals understand and uphold their own values. This course encourages participants to examine their personal ethics, recognize areas where they may not be acting in alignment with their values, and make adjustments that lead to greater self-respect and integrity. By gaining clarity on their principles, students become more consistent in their actions, allowing them to build stronger, more authentic relationships. Scientologists believe that developing personal integrity is a critical step in understanding oneself and interacting responsibly with others.

Another foundational course, the **Self Analysis Course**, offers tools for self-reflection and emotional clarity. In this course, students learn techniques for reviewing past experiences to understand how these memories affect their present behavior and feelings. By examining their thoughts and reactions, individuals develop a clearer understanding of what motivates them and how to make choices that lead to positive outcomes. Scientologists see this course as a pathway to increased emotional stability and self-awareness, as it encourages students to take control of their mental and emotional well-being.

The **Marriage Course** is also offered in many Scientology centers, aiming to improve understanding and communication within relationships. This course covers principles for building a stable, respectful partnership, focusing on trust, communication, and shared values. Through exercises that emphasize empathy and mutual respect, participants gain insights into how to strengthen their relationships and resolve conflicts constructively. Scientologists believe that understanding one's partner and addressing challenges openly are essential for maintaining healthy relationships.

For those interested in parenting, the **How to Improve Relationships with Children Course** provides insights into creating strong family bonds. This course covers communication techniques tailored for children, with exercises aimed at building trust and fostering open dialogue within the family. Participants learn strategies for handling conflicts constructively and supporting their child's emotional and social development. Scientologists view these skills as essential for creating a nurturing family environment where children feel respected and understood.

The **Ups and Downs in Life Course** addresses how to navigate challenges and handle difficult relationships. This course provides tools for recognizing negative influences, managing stressful situations, and maintaining personal stability in the face of adversity. Participants are encouraged to identify and mitigate factors that cause emotional distress or instability, leading to a more balanced and positive outlook. By learning to manage difficult situations effectively, students gain a better understanding of their own strengths and the power of resilience.

Each of these courses is designed to provide **practical tools for self-discovery and relationship building**, helping individuals improve their quality of life and their ability to connect with others. Scientologists believe that these skills not only enhance personal well-being but also support broader community goals, as effective communication, integrity, and resilience contribute to a more harmonious society.

## The Importance of Continuous Learning and Growth

Continuous learning is viewed as essential to personal and spiritual growth. The philosophy of ongoing education is woven into all aspects of Scientology training, encouraging individuals to seek knowledge and refine their skills throughout life. Scientologists believe that as one progresses on the Bridge to Total Freedom, new insights and challenges arise, making it important to continually expand understanding and improve abilities. Continuous learning is seen as the key to maintaining mental clarity, spiritual freedom, and effective interaction with the world.

One aspect of this commitment to ongoing growth is the **revisiting of foundational courses and skills**. Even experienced Scientologists return to early training materials and courses periodically, reviewing techniques and concepts to ensure they remain effective in their practice. This revisiting is not seen as redundancy but as a way to gain new insights from familiar teachings. With each return to foundational material, Scientologists report finding greater depth and relevance in concepts that might have initially seemed straightforward, allowing them to approach both personal challenges and auditing sessions with refreshed understanding.

Continuous learning in Scientology also involves **pursuing higher levels of training and auditing**. As individuals progress, they're encouraged to deepen their skills, particularly if they wish to support others on their spiritual journey. Advanced courses build on prior knowledge, helping individuals refine their ability to communicate, audit, and understand the complexities of the mind. By taking on new levels of training, Scientologists aim to not only enhance their own spiritual awareness but also contribute meaningfully to others' growth, as a trained auditor or mentor.

Scientology also encourages the practice of **self-reflection and personal assessment** as a way of identifying areas for improvement. Regular self-assessment helps individuals pinpoint aspects of their lives where they may have drifted from their goals or values. Scientologists are taught to look at challenges not as fixed obstacles but as opportunities for growth and insight. By regularly examining their progress and adjusting their course, they maintain alignment with their spiritual objectives, embracing learning as a lifelong endeavor that enriches both their own life and those of others.

The importance of continuous growth is embedded in Scientology's belief in **the Eight Dynamics**, where individuals are encouraged to not only improve themselves but also contribute positively to family, groups, society, and beyond. By continually seeking to learn and grow, Scientologists believe they can live more fulfilling lives and help create a more ethical, connected, and spiritually aware society.

## Specialized Training for Scientology Practitioners

For Scientology practitioners, specialized training offers advanced skills to support both personal spiritual growth and the progress of others on their journey through the Bridge. These training programs go beyond foundational courses, focusing on developing expertise in auditing and guiding others in Scientology practices. Practitioners undergo rigorous training to gain the proficiency needed to handle complex cases, which can involve deep-seated engrams or intense emotional experiences. Through this training, they prepare to take on greater responsibilities within the Church and to assist others in achieving mental clarity and spiritual awareness.

One specialized program is the **Class IV Auditor Course**, which certifies practitioners to conduct a range of auditing processes. At this level, trainees learn how to identify, handle, and process engrams effectively. The training emphasizes precision, ensuring that each auditor can create a safe and structured environment for the preclear to explore their past experiences and confront emotional barriers. Class IV auditors are also trained in maintaining neutrality and empathy, enabling them to support preclears without judgment, which is considered crucial for successful auditing sessions.

Another advanced training path involves the **Case Supervisor Training**. Case supervisors are responsible for overseeing the auditing process, providing guidance to auditors, and ensuring that each case progresses according to Scientology's principles. This role requires a deep understanding of the mind, auditing procedures, and the unique needs of each individual. Through specialized training, case supervisors learn how to review session notes, make recommendations for further auditing, and ensure that each preclear achieves optimal results. The case supervisor acts as a resource for auditors, offering insights and expertise to address complex cases effectively.

Scientology practitioners can also pursue training in **Advanced Clinical Courses (ACCs)**, which offer extensive instruction on handling specialized auditing situations and challenging cases. These courses are designed for experienced auditors looking to refine their techniques and broaden their understanding of the mind. ACCs cover advanced methods for guiding preclears through difficult experiences, exploring the deeper layers of the reactive mind, and addressing any barriers that might prevent spiritual progress. ACCs are particularly useful for auditors working with preclears who have already reached Clear and are advancing through the OT levels.

Some practitioners choose to specialize in **ministerial training** within Scientology. This path involves learning how to perform religious ceremonies, provide pastoral counseling, and offer spiritual guidance within the Scientology community. Ministerial training emphasizes ethical conduct, community involvement, and spiritual counseling techniques that align with Scientology's principles. Practitioners in this field are trained to support members in various aspects of life, including family issues, personal challenges, and spiritual questions, contributing to a well-rounded support system within the Church.

Through these specialized training paths, Scientology practitioners develop **skills that enable them to make a meaningful impact** within their community. Each training program is structured to provide the depth of knowledge and hands-on experience required for effective practice. Practitioners who complete specialized training are equipped to serve the Church in roles that support individuals on their spiritual journey, embodying Scientology's commitment to mental clarity, ethical conduct, and spiritual freedom.

## Certification and Recognition within Scientology

In Scientology, certification and recognition provide formal acknowledgment of a member's training, skills, and contributions. These achievements indicate a practitioner's dedication to learning and mastery of specific Scientology principles and practices, and they are important in maintaining high standards within the Church. Certification is granted upon the completion of various training levels, marking milestones in a practitioner's development. Through certification, Scientologists can take on roles that allow them to support and guide others, demonstrating their proficiency and commitment to Scientology's teachings.

One of the primary certifications in Scientology is the **Class IV Auditor certification**, which qualifies practitioners to audit preclears through a variety of processes. To receive this certification, individuals must complete rigorous training, mastering the techniques and ethics required to conduct effective auditing sessions. Class IV Auditors are recognized as capable of handling complex cases, and their certification represents a high level of trust within the Church. This certification allows them to work with preclears at different stages on the Bridge, supporting them in their journey toward Clear and beyond.

Practitioners who reach higher levels of auditing expertise may pursue certification as **Class V or Class VI Auditors**. These advanced certifications indicate proficiency in handling more complex auditing processes and cases involving preclears progressing through the Operating Thetan levels. Class V and VI Auditors are often involved in specialized cases, providing the technical skill and insight needed for advanced spiritual progress. This recognition allows them to take on greater responsibilities and work with individuals who require a more refined understanding of auditing techniques and spiritual guidance.

Certification in **Case Supervision** is also a significant achievement within Scientology. Case supervisors are responsible for overseeing the work of auditors, guiding them through complex cases, and ensuring that each preclear's journey is effective and ethical. Case supervisors must complete extensive training to understand all facets of auditing and to provide valuable feedback to auditors. This certification allows them to support both auditors and preclears, ensuring that each auditing session aligns with Scientology's principles and goals. The role of the case supervisor is highly respected, as it requires both technical knowledge and a deep commitment to the spiritual advancement of others.

Recognition within Scientology also extends to **ministerial roles**. Those who complete ministerial training receive certification as ordained ministers, enabling them to conduct ceremonies, provide pastoral counseling, and offer spiritual support to members of the community. Ministerial certification signifies a practitioner's readiness to serve in a spiritual leadership role, embodying the ethical standards and compassion expected within the Church. Ministers have a vital part in fostering a supportive community environment, addressing personal and spiritual needs, and representing Scientology's values in their interactions with others.

Scientology awards **acknowledgments and commendations** for practitioners who demonstrate excellence and dedication in their roles. These forms of recognition serve to highlight members' achievements and reinforce their contributions to the Church and its mission. By receiving these acknowledgments, practitioners gain a respected status within the community, inspiring others to pursue their own training and certifications. Through certifications, commendations, and formal recognition, Scientology builds a network of trained, capable individuals who work to uphold the standards of the Church and support its members' journey toward spiritual freedom.

# CHAPTER 10: SCIENTOLOGY ETHICS AND MORALITY

## The Code of Honor and Personal Integrity

In Scientology, the **Code of Honor** and **personal integrity** form the foundation of ethical behavior and moral strength. These principles guide individuals to make choices that reflect their values and align with the teachings of Scientology. The Code of Honor provides a set of guidelines that encourages responsible, honest, and ethical conduct, while personal integrity focuses on staying true to one's own beliefs and values without compromise.

The **Code of Honor** consists of 15 precepts that serve as a moral compass for Scientologists. It's designed to help individuals make choices that promote personal strength, trustworthiness, and respect for others. The code is not imposed but is followed voluntarily, reflecting the belief that true ethical behavior comes from within rather than external enforcement. Each precept emphasizes qualities like loyalty, truthfulness, and resilience, which Scientologists view as essential for living an honorable life. By adhering to the Code of Honor, individuals cultivate a sense of integrity and self-respect, knowing that they are acting in a way that aligns with their values.

One of the most important principles in the Code of Honor is **keeping one's word**. This precept underscores the importance of trust and reliability. Scientologists believe that a person's word is a reflection of their character; by honoring commitments, individuals build trust and demonstrate their integrity. Fulfilling promises is seen as essential to maintaining healthy relationships and establishing respect within the community. This commitment to honesty and reliability reinforces personal accountability, which is central to Scientology's ethical teachings.

Another key precept in the Code of Honor is the idea of **never compromising one's own beliefs or values**. Scientologists are encouraged to remain true to themselves and to avoid actions that conflict with their moral standards. This means resisting pressures to conform to the expectations of others if those expectations contradict their beliefs. By following this precept, Scientologists cultivate inner strength and resilience, learning to make choices based on their understanding of right and wrong. This commitment to personal integrity is considered essential for achieving a clear conscience and genuine self-respect.

**Respect for others' beliefs and rights** is also emphasized within the Code of Honor. Scientologists are taught to honor the beliefs of others, even if they differ from their own. This respect is seen as essential for fostering a harmonious community where individuals feel valued and understood. By upholding this principle, Scientologists aim to build a society based on mutual respect and empathy, where individuals can express themselves freely. This respect for diversity aligns with Scientology's emphasis on understanding and compassion.

Alongside the Code of Honor, **personal integrity** is viewed as a vital aspect of a Scientologist's moral foundation. Personal integrity in Scientology means staying true to one's own sense of right and wrong, acting in ways that align with personal values, and being honest with oneself. It's not just about adhering to rules or expectations; it's about making choices that reflect an individual's core beliefs and principles. Personal integrity is seen as the basis for true ethical conduct because it ensures that actions are guided by genuine understanding rather than compliance.

Scientologists are encouraged to regularly **examine their own thoughts and actions** to ensure they align with their values. This practice of self-reflection supports personal integrity by helping individuals stay aware of their choices and motivations. By reflecting on their actions, Scientologists gain a clearer understanding of their intentions and how these intentions affect others. This self-awareness is essential for personal growth, as it helps individuals identify areas where they may need to adjust their behavior to stay aligned with their values.

**Admitting mistakes and taking responsibility** is another critical aspect of personal integrity. In Scientology, individuals are taught that acknowledging errors and learning from them is a sign of strength, not weakness. By taking responsibility for their actions, Scientologists reinforce their commitment to ethical conduct and demonstrate their willingness to grow. This approach builds trust and self-respect, as individuals learn to face challenges openly rather than avoiding accountability. This focus on responsibility is also considered crucial for maintaining strong relationships and contributing positively to the community.

Through both the Code of Honor and personal integrity, Scientology encourages individuals to **act consistently with their principles** and to take responsibility for their decisions. These practices promote personal empowerment, as individuals are able to stand confidently by their beliefs and make choices that align with their values. The combination of the Code of Honor's guidelines and the emphasis on personal integrity fosters a moral foundation that supports personal strength, resilience, and respect for others.

For Scientologists, the Code of Honor and personal integrity aren't just ideals; they're practical approaches to living an ethical and fulfilling life. They help individuals navigate challenges, make responsible choices, and build trust within their communities. By following these principles, Scientologists work toward creating a society where individuals can live authentically, respect each other, and contribute to a positive, supportive environment.

# Scientology's Ethics System and Procedures

Scientology's **ethics system** is structured to support individual and collective integrity, helping members align their actions with Scientology's principles and values. This system isn't simply about following rules; it's a framework designed to help individuals make decisions that enhance their personal well-being and contribute positively to the community. Central to the ethics system is the idea that each person has an inherent responsibility for their actions and the impact they have on others. Through training and courses, Scientologists are introduced to specific ethics procedures that they can use to assess and improve their own behavior and contribute to a more ethical society.

The ethics system includes **various procedures and tools**, which Scientologists learn in dedicated ethics courses. These courses cover concepts like conditions of existence, which outline different levels of ethical standing or "conditions" that individuals can find themselves in, based on their actions. Conditions range from Confusion to Power, each representing a level of alignment with Scientology's values. Scientologists learn about these conditions to understand where they currently stand and to gain clarity on how they can improve their ethical status. By identifying their condition, members can follow a prescribed series of steps to move toward more stable, constructive behavior.

One essential part of the ethics system is **the Conditions Formulae**, a set of specific actions that apply to each condition. Each formula contains steps designed to help individuals regain stability and improve their circumstances. For instance, someone who finds themselves in the condition of Doubt may work through a Doubt Formula, a series of questions and actions that guide them in examining their current situation and making decisions to resolve their doubts. Through ethics training, Scientologists practice applying these formulas, allowing them to navigate ethical challenges with a structured, proactive approach.

Another key component of the ethics system is the **use of Knowledge Reports**. When Scientologists observe behavior within the community that goes against the values of Scientology, they can write a Knowledge Report detailing the issue. These reports are not meant to shame or punish but to encourage responsibility and transparency. Through the ethics system, Knowledge Reports are used to address ethical breaches in a way that supports the individual's growth. Scientology courses on ethics teach members how to write and process these reports respectfully, focusing on constructive solutions rather than assigning blame.

The ethics system also includes **ethics officers** who help guide members in applying ethical principles. These officers are trained to help Scientologists work through personal challenges, resolve conflicts, and align their actions with Scientology's values. Ethics officers assist individuals in understanding their current condition, applying appropriate formulas, and taking corrective steps if necessary. Their role is to provide support, not punishment, as the goal of the ethics system is to restore ethical behavior and personal integrity. Scientology's training courses emphasize the role of ethics officers as mentors who promote self-improvement and accountability.

Through **ethics training**, Scientologists also learn about the role of ethics in spiritual growth. Courses often highlight the connection between ethical behavior and progress on the Bridge to Total Freedom. Scientologists are taught that ethical lapses can create barriers to spiritual advancement, as unresolved issues can cloud one's mind and hinder progress. By maintaining ethical conduct, individuals keep their path clear, enabling smoother advancement through auditing and training. This emphasis on ethics as a foundational element of spiritual progress reinforces the idea that personal growth and ethical behavior are deeply interconnected.

Scientology's ethics courses cover **conflict resolution techniques**, which are applied when misunderstandings or disputes arise within the community. Members learn tools for communicating openly, addressing issues respectfully, and working toward mutually beneficial outcomes. Conflict resolution is seen as an essential skill, especially for auditors and other practitioners who regularly interact with others in emotionally sensitive situations. Through these courses, Scientologists learn to handle conflicts constructively, aligning their approach with the principles of mutual respect and understanding.

Training in the ethics system prepares members to take responsibility for their actions, recognize the impact of their choices, and make conscious efforts to improve. By learning these ethics procedures, Scientologists gain tools to assess and adjust their behavior in alignment with the values of Scientology, ultimately supporting both their own progress and the integrity of the community.

## Maintaining and Restoring Ethical Behavior

In Scientology, maintaining ethical behavior is essential for personal and spiritual progress, and it's supported through structured training and courses. Scientologists are taught that consistent ethical behavior keeps them aligned with their values, promoting a state of stability and mental clarity. **Ethics courses** provide tools and techniques for staying on course, allowing individuals to identify and address potential ethical lapses before they become significant issues. By understanding the importance of ethics, members gain insight into how their actions impact themselves and others, reinforcing the value of consistent ethical conduct.

**Self-assessment techniques** are a core component of maintaining ethical behavior. In ethics training, Scientologists learn to regularly evaluate their actions, thoughts, and motivations. This self-assessment process involves examining one's current condition and applying the appropriate Conditions Formula to ensure alignment with Scientology's values. By using self-assessment, individuals can address minor issues before they escalate, keeping their path clear and supporting ongoing personal and spiritual growth. Regular self-assessment is viewed as essential for maintaining personal integrity and consistency in one's actions.

When ethical behavior needs restoration, Scientologists turn to **ethics correction steps** learned in training. These correction steps guide individuals in identifying the root causes of their actions and making amends. For example, someone who has found themselves in a state of Doubt might work through the Doubt Formula, analyzing the situation and taking specific steps to restore their ethical standing. Restoration procedures are designed not as punishment but as tools for growth, allowing members to regain stability and improve their circumstances. Through ethics courses, Scientologists practice applying these steps to ensure they can handle ethical challenges effectively.

**Conflict resolution skills** taught in ethics training are also crucial for maintaining ethical behavior within the Scientology community. Members learn methods for addressing misunderstandings and resolving disputes, which is especially valuable in maintaining positive relationships and a harmonious environment. By applying these skills, individuals work through conflicts constructively, focusing on solutions rather than assigning blame. Training in conflict resolution helps prevent ethical breaches caused by misunderstandings or unresolved issues, ensuring that Scientologists can communicate openly and address challenges respectfully.

**Accountability and transparency** are emphasized throughout ethics training. Scientologists are taught to accept responsibility for their actions and to be honest about their mistakes. By fostering an environment of accountability, the Church encourages members to address ethical challenges directly, without fear of judgment. This approach supports a culture of continuous improvement, where individuals feel empowered to make positive changes. Transparency is encouraged through practices like Knowledge Reports, allowing individuals to address concerns constructively and keep the community aligned with Scientology's values.

## Consequences of Ethical Violations

Ethical violations are addressed with a focus on personal responsibility and corrective action rather than punishment. When ethical breaches occur, Scientologists are encouraged to take responsibility and work through specific corrective steps learned in training. Through **ethics courses**, members are taught to view these consequences as opportunities for growth, helping individuals recognize the impact of their actions and learn from their mistakes. Scientologists believe that addressing ethical violations constructively allows individuals to restore integrity and continue their spiritual journey on a clear path.

When an ethical violation occurs, Scientologists often engage in the **Conditions Formulae** to determine the appropriate steps for recovery. For example, if someone's actions have placed them in a condition of Liability, they are encouraged to work through the Liability Formula. This formula involves acknowledging the situation, taking responsibility, and making amends with those affected. Ethics courses teach members to apply these formulas effectively, guiding them in the process of addressing their actions and restoring ethical behavior. By following these steps, individuals demonstrate their commitment to improvement, reinforcing trust within the community.

Consequences for ethical violations may also include **formal ethics interviews** with ethics officers. These officers are trained to help individuals understand their current condition, assess their actions, and determine the corrective steps needed to restore alignment with Scientology's values. Ethics officers work with individuals to apply relevant Conditions Formulae and support them in taking responsibility. This process is seen as a collaborative effort to help members regain stability and integrity, rather than as a form of punishment. Scientologists are taught that ethics officers are there to provide guidance and encouragement, helping individuals resolve issues constructively.

**Knowledge Reports** are another tool used when addressing ethical violations. If a member observes behavior that appears to violate Scientology's ethical principles, they may submit a Knowledge Report to bring attention to the matter. Knowledge Reports are not used to shame or judge; instead, they serve as a way to identify and resolve ethical concerns in a constructive manner. Through ethics training, members learn how to write and respond to Knowledge Reports in a respectful way, focusing on corrective actions that restore integrity and support personal growth.

In cases of repeated or severe ethical violations, **corrective measures** may include a temporary restriction from certain Church activities. This restriction is not intended as punishment but as a way to encourage the individual to focus on addressing their ethical standing. Through ethics courses, Scientologists learn that these measures are a form of support, helping individuals gain clarity on their actions and make necessary changes. Once corrective steps are completed and ethical behavior is restored, the individual can fully reintegrate into Church activities.

The emphasis on **personal responsibility and constructive correction** in Scientology's ethics system reflects the Church's commitment to helping members learn from their experiences. Rather than focusing on punitive measures, Scientology encourages individuals to view consequences as learning opportunities. This approach to ethical violations supports a culture of growth, where individuals are empowered to make amends, rebuild trust, and continue their spiritual journey with renewed integrity.

# CHAPTER 11: THE PURIFICATION RUNDOWN

## Purpose and Benefits of the Purification Rundown

The **Purification Rundown** is a unique program in Scientology designed to help individuals rid their bodies of toxins and impurities that can impact their mental clarity and spiritual awareness. L. Ron Hubbard developed this regimen to address the belief that chemicals, pollutants, and other toxic substances accumulate in the body over time, potentially clouding the mind and obstructing spiritual progress. Scientologists believe that by eliminating these residues, a person can achieve a clearer mind, experience increased energy, and improve their overall well-being.

One of the main purposes of the Purification Rundown is to **enhance mental clarity**. Scientologists are taught that accumulated toxins, including drugs and chemicals, can remain lodged in the body's tissues, particularly fat cells, and continue to influence the mind long after initial exposure. These lingering residues are believed to interfere with mental clarity, creating a "fog" that makes it difficult to focus, think clearly, and maintain emotional stability. The Purification Rundown is intended to flush these substances out of the system, allowing individuals to regain mental sharpness and experience life with a fresh perspective. By completing the Rundown, Scientologists aim to clear away these barriers to mental clarity, which they see as essential for spiritual growth.

Another significant purpose of the Purification Rundown is to help individuals **recover from the long-term effects of drug and substance use**. Many people who enter the Rundown have previously used drugs or been exposed to environmental pollutants, which Scientologists believe can leave lasting residues in the body. These residues are thought to create cravings, impact physical health, and affect emotional well-being. By completing the Rundown, participants work to eliminate these lingering effects, which allows them to regain control over their physical and emotional health. Scientologists view this as a way to free themselves from the influence of past drug use and make a fresh start, both physically and spiritually.

The **Purification Rundown is structured around a specific regimen** of exercise, sauna sessions, and nutrition. Participants engage in daily physical exercise, such as running, to stimulate circulation and promote the release of toxins. This exercise component is intended to activate the body's natural detoxification processes, helping to mobilize residues stored in tissues. Alongside exercise, participants spend extended periods in a sauna, where sweating is believed to help expel toxins from the body. The idea is that sweat carries out impurities, allowing the body to cleanse itself more effectively. By combining exercise and sauna sessions, the Rundown is thought to work holistically to remove harmful substances from the body.

Nutrition also has a key role in the Rundown. Participants are encouraged to follow a specific regimen of vitamins and minerals, with particular emphasis on high doses of **niacin (vitamin B3)**. In Scientology, niacin is thought to help release stored toxins, especially from fat cells. The Purification Rundown uses high doses of this vitamin, along with other supplements, to support the detoxification process. Participants are also advised to follow a healthy diet to ensure they're receiving essential nutrients, which is believed to aid the body's ability to process and remove toxins effectively. The focus on nutrition reinforces the idea that proper dietary support is necessary for optimal health and detoxification.

One of the key **benefits of the Purification Rundown** is improved physical energy and stamina. Scientologists believe that toxins in the body can sap energy and contribute to feelings of lethargy or fatigue. By eliminating these substances, participants report feeling more energized, alert, and capable of handling daily activities with renewed vigor. This increase in energy is seen as not just a physical benefit but as a stepping stone to achieving more in life. Scientologists consider this heightened energy essential for pursuing their goals and responsibilities with clarity and enthusiasm.

The Rundown is also intended to **enhance emotional stability**. Scientologists believe that toxic residues can create emotional imbalances, leading to irritability, mood swings, and even depression. By removing these residues, participants often report experiencing a greater sense of emotional calm and resilience. This emotional stability is viewed as beneficial not only for the individual but also for their interactions with others, as it allows them to engage with people from a place of balance and understanding. Scientologists see this as a way to improve relationships and foster a supportive community, as individuals are better able to communicate and connect without being influenced by emotional turbulence.

Beyond physical and emotional improvements, the Purification Rundown is thought to **promote spiritual clarity**. Scientologists believe that a body burdened with toxins can obscure spiritual perception, creating barriers that prevent individuals from fully experiencing their spiritual nature. By completing the Rundown, they aim to achieve a state of purity that allows for deeper spiritual connection and insight. This clarity is considered vital for progressing through the stages on the Bridge to Total Freedom, as it creates a foundation for further spiritual exploration. With a cleansed body and clearer mind, individuals are believed to be more receptive to the insights and awareness that come with Scientology practices.

Finally, the Rundown offers **a renewed sense of control and responsibility over one's health**. Completing the Rundown requires commitment and discipline, and many participants view it as a turning point in taking charge of their well-being. By investing in this process, they feel empowered to make healthier choices, reduce their exposure to harmful substances, and adopt habits that support long-term health. This commitment to health is seen as an important part of the Scientology journey, as it reflects a proactive approach to life and spiritual growth.

Through the Purification Rundown, Scientologists strive to create a body and mind that are free of toxic influences, enabling them to live with greater clarity, resilience, and spiritual openness.

## Detoxification Processes and Techniques

The Purification Rundown incorporates a structured regimen of **detoxification techniques** aimed at removing accumulated toxins from the body. These processes are intended to clear the physical system of residues from drugs, pollutants, and other environmental substances that may have lasting effects on physical and mental well-being. Scientologists believe that by following these processes, participants can cleanse their bodies thoroughly, allowing for a renewed sense of clarity and vitality.

A core component of the detoxification process is **sauna therapy**, which involves extended periods in a sauna each day. Scientologists believe that sweating in a heated environment encourages the release of toxins from fat cells, where these residues are thought to accumulate. By stimulating sweat production, the sauna helps participants expel harmful substances through their pores, releasing toxins that are stored deep within the body's tissues. Daily sauna sessions are an essential part of the Rundown, as they are believed to support the body's natural detoxification systems in a way that regular activities cannot achieve on their own.

**Exercise** is another fundamental technique used in the Purification Rundown to mobilize toxins in the body. Participants engage in physical activities like running to increase circulation, improve cardiovascular health, and stimulate the body's metabolic processes. Scientologists hold that exercise accelerates the movement of blood and lymph fluids, which helps to carry toxins from storage sites within the body to areas where they can be eliminated. Physical activity in combination with sauna therapy is seen as enhancing the detoxification process, as exercise activates circulation while the sauna helps release toxins from the skin.

As mentioned, a key aspect of the detoxification process in the Rundown is the use of **high doses of niacin (vitamin B3)**. When taken in specific quantities, niacin is thought to trigger a "flushing" effect, increasing blood flow to the skin and creating a sensation of warmth. This effect is believed to help mobilize toxins stored in fat deposits, making them easier to eliminate through sweating. The Purification Rundown uses this "niacin flush" as a way to intensify the detox process, helping the body rid itself of residues that may otherwise remain stored indefinitely.

In addition to niacin, the Rundown incorporates a regimen of **other vitamins and minerals**. Scientologists believe that supplements like vitamins A, C, D, and E, as well as minerals like calcium and magnesium, help support the body's detox functions by replenishing essential nutrients and boosting immunity. These supplements are taken alongside niacin and aim to provide a balanced approach to detoxification, enhancing the body's resilience while counteracting potential deficiencies that may arise during the detox process. This nutritional support is seen as crucial to the overall efficacy of the Rundown, as it provides the body with the resources it needs to handle the detoxification demands.

Throughout the Purification Rundown, participants are encouraged to drink plenty of **water and electrolyte-rich beverages**. Hydration is considered essential for the effectiveness of the detoxification process, as fluids help to flush out toxins through sweat and urine. Scientologists believe that water intake prevents dehydration, which could hinder the body's ability to release stored toxins. Electrolytes are also incorporated to maintain balance, as the combination of exercise, sauna, and high fluid intake can deplete minerals necessary for muscle function and energy levels.

## Enhancing Spiritual Awareness Through Physical Health

In Scientology, physical health is closely tied to **spiritual awareness**. The Purification Rundown is viewed as a process that not only cleanses the body but also creates the conditions necessary for heightened spiritual sensitivity. Scientologists believe that when the body is burdened with toxins and residues from drugs and pollutants, it can impede a person's ability to connect with their true spiritual self. By purifying the body, they aim to clear away physical obstructions that might otherwise inhibit spiritual insight and awareness.

Scientologists consider the body to be an **instrument for spiritual experience**. Just as a clear lens allows one to see sharply, a cleansed body is thought to allow for a more vivid spiritual perception. When toxins are removed from the body, Scientologists believe that the mind becomes less clouded, enabling individuals to connect more deeply with their inner consciousness. This physical purification is seen as essential for anyone seeking to advance on the Bridge to Total Freedom, as it prepares the individual for the spiritual demands of the journey by creating an unobstructed pathway between the physical and spiritual realms.

Through the Rundown, participants often report an increased **sensitivity to their environment and experiences**. This heightened perception is believed to be a result of the body's renewed health and clarity, which Scientologists see as removing barriers that may have dulled awareness. By enhancing the body's vitality, individuals become more attuned to the subtleties of their surroundings, emotions, and thoughts. This enhanced awareness is seen as a crucial step for spiritual growth, as it allows individuals to better understand themselves and their relationship with the world.

Scientologists believe that enhancing physical health through the Rundown creates a **supportive foundation for mental and spiritual practices**, such as auditing and training. When the body is free of toxic residues, the mind is seen as more receptive to learning, self-exploration, and introspection. The Rundown is thought to prepare individuals for these practices by promoting a stable and resilient state of mind, one that is better equipped to engage in the deeper levels of spiritual work required by Scientology.

**Emotional resilience** is also considered a benefit of this approach. Scientologists believe that a cleansed body contributes to emotional stability, which is seen as essential for spiritual exploration. When the body is free of substances that may cause mood swings or irritability, individuals can approach their spiritual journey with a calm and open mind. This emotional balance, achieved through physical purification, is thought to facilitate a more meaningful engagement with the teachings and experiences of Scientology.

## Diet and Lifestyle Considerations in Purification

Diet and lifestyle choices are critical components of the Purification Rundown, as they support the body's ability to **detoxify and rejuvenate**. Scientologists following the Rundown are advised to adopt specific dietary practices that provide the necessary nutrients for a rigorous detoxification process. Nutrient-dense foods are encouraged, as they supply essential vitamins and minerals that help counterbalance the demands placed on the body during the Rundown. Fresh fruits, vegetables, whole grains, and lean proteins are typically emphasized to support the body's health and stamina.

Avoiding **processed foods, sugars, and artificial additives** is also recommended, as these are seen as sources of additional toxins that could hinder the detox process. Scientologists believe that minimizing the intake of processed foods helps reduce the body's toxic load, allowing the detoxification methods used in the Rundown to work more effectively. This focus on whole, unprocessed foods is thought to support digestion and enhance nutrient absorption, giving the body the resources it needs to handle the demands of sauna sessions and exercise.

The Purification Rundown also encourages the **use of natural, organic products** whenever possible. Scientologists believe that choosing organic foods and avoiding chemically-laden products can reduce the introduction of new toxins into the body. By focusing on clean, natural sources of nutrition, participants aim to create an environment in the body that's less burdened by synthetic substances. This approach is believed to complement the Rundown's goal of removing pre-existing residues, as it helps to prevent additional impurities from accumulating during the detox process.

Lifestyle adjustments during the Rundown include maintaining **regular hydration** to support the body's cleansing processes. Participants are encouraged to drink water throughout the day to assist in flushing out toxins mobilized during sauna sessions and exercise. Hydration helps support the kidneys, liver, and skin—all key organs in the detoxification process—by facilitating the removal of residues through sweat and urine. Scientologists see hydration as an essential part of maintaining the body's balance and energy levels, especially as detoxification demands increase.

**Adequate rest and sleep** are also prioritized during the Rundown, as Scientologists believe that rest is necessary for the body's regenerative processes. Detoxification can be taxing, and rest allows the body to recover and continue releasing toxins effectively. Participants are encouraged to create a calm environment that supports relaxation and sleep, ensuring their body is prepared for each day's activities on the Rundown. By prioritizing rest, they aim to maximize the body's ability to cleanse and maintain stability throughout the detox process.

Limiting exposure to **environmental toxins** is another lifestyle consideration during the Rundown. Participants are advised to avoid areas with high levels of pollution, smoke, or chemicals, as these could counteract the detoxification efforts. Scientologists believe that by minimizing exposure to environmental toxins, participants can protect the progress made through the Rundown and help maintain a cleaner physical state. These lifestyle considerations are seen as necessary for keeping the body's detoxification pathways open and functioning effectively, aligning the individual's daily life with the goals of the Purification Rundown.

# CHAPTER 12: THE ROLE OF COMMUNICATION

## The Importance of Effective Communication

In Scientology, **effective communication** is considered essential for personal development, understanding others, and achieving a state of mental clarity. Scientologists view communication as more than just exchanging words; it's a means of connecting with others on a deeper level and understanding their viewpoints. Effective communication enables individuals to express themselves clearly, resolve misunderstandings, and build trust. Scientology teaches that mastering this skill is fundamental to progressing on the Bridge to Total Freedom.

**One of the core principles of communication in Scientology** is the concept of reaching. To truly communicate, one must reach out, intending to connect with the other person. This reaching is about focusing one's attention fully on the person they're speaking to and ensuring that their message is fully received. Scientologists believe that real communication happens when both parties are fully engaged and willing to understand each other. This creates a space where ideas can be shared without distraction, allowing each person to fully absorb what the other is saying.

**Listening is equally important.** In Scientology, listening is not passive; it's an active process that involves giving one's full attention and understanding the speaker's perspective. Effective listening requires patience, focus, and an openness to receive without immediate judgment or interruption. Scientologists learn that true listening goes beyond hearing words—it involves recognizing emotions, intentions, and the context behind the message. This approach creates mutual understanding and respect, which are seen as the foundations of any constructive interaction.

To support effective communication, Scientology emphasizes the importance of **acknowledgment**. Acknowledging someone's communication shows that you have heard and understood them. Simple responses like "I see," "I understand," or even a nod can make the other person feel validated and respected. Acknowledgment is seen as essential because it assures the speaker that their message has been received, helping to prevent misunderstandings and build rapport. Scientologists view acknowledgment as a way to close the cycle of communication, reinforcing the connection between individuals.

**Clarity in expression** is also central to effective communication in Scientology. To be understood, one must communicate their thoughts and feelings clearly and concisely. Scientologists are taught to avoid vagueness or ambiguity in their language, as unclear communication can lead to confusion and misinterpretation. When people speak with clarity, they eliminate unnecessary barriers and allow for a more direct, meaningful exchange. Clarity not only benefits the person being spoken to but also helps the speaker organize their own thoughts and intentions, contributing to greater self-awareness.

In Scientology, **communication exercises** are used to develop these skills. Drills known as "Training Routines" (TRs) are practiced to improve concentration, self-control, and the ability to handle communication challenges. One basic exercise involves sitting face-to-face with another person, maintaining eye contact without reacting to distractions. This exercise, known as TR 0, teaches individuals to be fully present and comfortable in another's presence. By practicing TR 0, Scientologists learn to control their attention and remain focused on the interaction, which is seen as the foundation of effective communication.

Other communication exercises, like **TR 1**, involve practicing the clear delivery of a message without hesitation or overemphasis. This exercise helps Scientologists develop the ability to speak directly and confidently, without unnecessary fillers or hesitations. Practicing TR 1 allows individuals to refine their delivery, ensuring that their message is received as intended. Scientologists see this skill as essential for effective communication, as it fosters confidence and helps the speaker maintain control over their own expression.

Scientology also emphasizes the importance of **handling and resolving communication barriers**. Barriers to communication can arise from many sources, including assumptions, biases, emotional responses, and distractions. Through training, Scientologists learn to identify and address these barriers, helping to ensure that interactions remain constructive and focused. For instance, someone might learn techniques for staying calm in the face of criticism or handling misunderstandings without becoming defensive. This ability to manage communication barriers is seen as essential for maintaining effective relationships and resolving conflicts.

In addition, Scientology teaches that **effective communication is vital for self-discovery**. By engaging in open, honest dialogue with others, individuals can gain insights into their own thoughts and feelings. Scientologists believe that communication acts as a mirror, reflecting one's own mind and revealing areas for personal growth. Engaging in clear and sincere communication can help individuals identify beliefs, habits, or fears that may have been hidden. This self-discovery process is seen as a key part of spiritual advancement, as it allows individuals to confront and work through internal barriers.

Effective communication also extends beyond words to include **nonverbal cues**, such as facial expressions, body language, and tone of voice. Scientologists are taught to be aware of their own nonverbal signals and to observe those of others. These nonverbal cues often carry as much meaning as spoken words and can influence how a message is received. By developing an awareness of nonverbal communication, individuals can enhance their ability to express themselves authentically and understand others more fully. Scientologists believe that a person's presence and demeanor contribute significantly to their communication effectiveness, allowing for a more genuine connection.

In interpersonal relationships, **effective communication fosters trust and empathy**. Scientologists learn that when people communicate openly and with respect, they can resolve conflicts, share ideas, and create a foundation of trust. This trust allows individuals to support one another, share experiences, and build lasting relationships. Effective communication is seen as a powerful tool for creating harmony within families, groups, and communities. By applying the communication skills taught in Scientology, individuals are encouraged to strengthen their connections and make a positive impact on the people around them.

Through training and practice, Scientologists develop effective communication skills that serve them in all areas of life. From personal relationships to professional settings, they see communication as the bridge that connects people, enables understanding, and promotes personal growth.

## Drills and Techniques to Improve Communication

Communication drills and techniques are used to develop and refine the essential skills needed for clear, confident, and effective communication. Known as **Training Routines** (TRs), these drills are designed to help individuals become more aware of their responses, focus their attention, and improve their ability to communicate purposefully and without distraction. Each drill builds on specific aspects of communication, allowing Scientologists to practice and gain control over their interactions in a structured way.

The **first drill, TR 0**, involves sitting face-to-face with a partner, maintaining direct eye contact, and remaining still and focused. This exercise is sometimes referred to as "being there" comfortably in another person's presence. The goal of TR 0 is to increase awareness and self-control, allowing the individual to be present without reacting to distractions or physical discomfort. Practicing this drill helps Scientologists become more comfortable in any situation, learning to control their attention and remain composed. Scientologists believe that by mastering this ability to stay grounded and fully present, individuals build a foundation for effective communication.

**TR 1**, known as "Dear Alice," focuses on the **delivery of a message**. In this drill, participants read lines from "Alice in Wonderland" or another source, practicing clear, direct communication with their partner. The purpose is to ensure that the message is delivered exactly as intended, without hesitation or excessive emotion. By practicing TR 1, Scientologists learn to communicate their thoughts confidently and concisely, without letting personal reactions or external influences interfere. This drill helps individuals control their tone, pace, and clarity, which are essential elements for conveying any message effectively.

**TR 2** is an exercise in **acknowledgment**. In this drill, participants respond to their partner's statements with simple, genuine acknowledgments like "Thank you," "I understand," or a brief nod. The goal of TR 2 is to practice making others feel heard and validated. Scientologists believe that acknowledgment is a vital part of the communication cycle, as it completes the exchange and ensures that the speaker feels understood. By mastering this drill, participants learn to listen actively and respond appropriately, reinforcing the speaker's confidence in their communication.

In **TR 3**, known as **"repetition,"** the participant asks a question repeatedly until they receive a satisfactory answer. The exercise trains individuals to stay focused on their question and not deviate, even if the partner attempts to change the subject or distract them. TR 3 helps develop persistence and the ability to keep a conversation on track, ensuring that important questions or points aren't left unanswered. This drill is particularly useful in situations that require clarity and directness, such as clarifying instructions or handling challenging conversations.

**TR 4**, called "Handling Originations," teaches participants to respond appropriately to unexpected statements or emotions from their partner. In this drill, the partner may say something off-topic or emotional, and the participant practices acknowledging and addressing the statement without losing focus on the original topic. This exercise helps Scientologists develop flexibility in communication, teaching them to handle unexpected responses or emotions without becoming reactive. TR 4 is valuable in real-life situations where unexpected issues or emotions may arise, allowing individuals to respond calmly and stay on course.

**Advanced TRs**, like "Upper Indoctrination TRs," take these skills further by simulating more challenging communication scenarios. These drills involve additional layers of distraction or emotional complexity, pushing participants to maintain control over their responses even under pressure. Scientologists believe these advanced drills build resilience and confidence, preparing individuals to communicate effectively in high-stress or emotionally charged situations. By mastering these techniques, participants can engage in difficult conversations while maintaining clarity, empathy, and control.

**Object Drills** are also used to strengthen observation and descriptive skills. In these drills, participants describe objects in great detail, focusing on color, shape, texture, and other characteristics. This practice sharpens attention to detail and encourages individuals to express themselves clearly and precisely. Object Drills help Scientologists become more descriptive and focused in their communication, allowing them to convey ideas in a way that's easy for others to understand.

Through these drills, Scientologists develop both the foundational skills and the nuanced techniques required for effective communication. The goal is not only to master communication techniques but also to gain control over one's own reactions and expressions. Scientologists believe that by becoming adept at these drills, individuals can approach any conversation with confidence, maintain composure, and ensure that their messages are delivered and understood as intended.

# Communication and Understanding in Relationships

Communication is viewed as the foundation for healthy, understanding-based relationships in scientology. Effective communication allows individuals to express their feelings, share perspectives, and address conflicts constructively. Scientologists believe that communication is not just about talking; it's about creating a real connection between people, fostering mutual respect and understanding. This approach is applied in personal relationships, family dynamics, and friendships, with the idea that understanding one another's thoughts and emotions builds trust and stability.

One of the principles taught in Scientology for relationships is the **importance of open and honest communication**. In a relationship, each person is encouraged to express themselves fully and to communicate openly about their thoughts, feelings, and intentions. Scientologists believe that honest communication is essential for building trust and preventing misunderstandings. When individuals share their thoughts without withholding or concealing information, they create a relationship based on authenticity and respect. Open communication helps both parties understand each other's motivations and goals, which Scientologists see as vital for maintaining a balanced and harmonious relationship.

In relationships, **listening has an equally important role** as speaking. Scientologists learn that to truly understand a partner or friend, one must listen with full attention, without interrupting or reacting impulsively. Listening is viewed as an active process that requires patience and empathy. When individuals listen carefully, they allow the speaker to feel valued and understood, which strengthens the connection between them. Effective listening can defuse conflicts, as it allows both parties to feel that their concerns are acknowledged and respected.

**Acknowledgment** is another key aspect of maintaining understanding in relationships. Scientologists are taught that acknowledgment confirms to the speaker that they've been heard and understood, completing the communication cycle. Simple acknowledgments, such as nodding, saying "I see" or "I understand," show the other person that their words are taken seriously. This process fosters trust and assures both parties that they are on the same page. By consistently practicing acknowledgment, Scientologists create a space where open dialogue can flourish, enhancing mutual respect.

Scientologists also learn techniques for **resolving conflicts through communication**. When disagreements arise, the goal is to address them constructively, without blame or defensiveness. Scientologists are encouraged to communicate their own perspectives clearly and to listen to the other person's side without interruption. By staying calm and respectful, both parties can work toward a solution that respects each other's viewpoints. Conflict resolution is seen as an opportunity to strengthen relationships, as it allows individuals to confront issues directly and come to a deeper understanding of each other's needs.

**Communication in relationships also involves empathy**, which means understanding and sharing the feelings of others. In Scientology, empathy is considered essential for creating strong, supportive bonds. Practicing empathy allows individuals to respond to others with kindness and patience, which fosters trust and emotional safety. When one partner empathizes with the other's experiences, it builds a foundation of support and understanding that enhances the relationship.

Another approach Scientologists use to strengthen relationships is the concept of **matching communication styles**. They believe that adjusting one's communication style to suit the other person's preferences can help facilitate understanding. For instance, if one person prefers direct, concise communication, the other can mirror that style to ensure their message is received as intended. This approach shows consideration for the other person's preferences and creates a smoother interaction.

Scientologists emphasize that **effective communication is ongoing**. Regular check-ins, open dialogue, and honest sharing keep relationships strong and adaptable. By consistently communicating, individuals address small issues before they grow into larger problems, keeping the relationship balanced and healthy. Scientologists believe that this continuous, mindful communication fosters understanding and helps relationships adapt to changes and challenges over time. Through intentional communication practices, relationships in Scientology are nurtured, grounded in respect, empathy, and genuine connection.

## The Impact of Communication on Self-Awareness

In Scientology, communication is not only a tool for connecting with others but also a means of developing self-awareness. By expressing thoughts, beliefs, and emotions openly, individuals gain insight into their own minds, understanding their motivations and identifying patterns in their behavior. Scientologists believe that each interaction is an opportunity for self-reflection, allowing people to confront aspects of themselves that may not be immediately visible without verbalization. Communication thus serves as a mirror, reflecting one's inner world and helping uncover insights essential for personal growth.

Through structured communication exercises, Scientologists learn to **observe their own reactions and responses**. When individuals pay attention to how they respond in conversations, they begin to see habitual patterns, automatic reactions, or even hidden emotions that might otherwise go unnoticed. For example, someone might discover a tendency to interrupt or become defensive in certain situations. By recognizing these patterns, they gain awareness of areas where they may want to improve, fostering greater self-control and adaptability.

Self-awareness in communication is also cultivated by **acknowledging the emotions that arise during interactions**. Scientologists practice noticing and labeling their feelings in real-time, whether it's frustration, excitement, or impatience. Recognizing these emotional states helps individuals understand what triggers specific reactions and allows them to respond more consciously. This emotional insight enables them to take a step back, assess the situation objectively, and choose actions that align with their values rather than impulsively reacting. Over time, this awareness helps individuals develop a stable and balanced approach to communication, rooted in clarity rather than emotional reactivity.

In Scientology, **reflective listening** is another technique that deepens self-awareness. By repeating or paraphrasing what another person says, individuals can better gauge their own understanding and feelings about the topic. This practice not only ensures that they comprehend the speaker's message but also reveals any biases or assumptions that might color their interpretation. Scientologists see reflective listening as a way to confront their own preconceptions, which can limit the ability to understand others accurately. Becoming aware of these biases through communication allows for greater mental clarity and encourages a more genuine connection with others.

Another way communication enhances self-awareness in Scientology is by **revealing one's personal beliefs and values**. When individuals discuss topics important to them, they articulate and refine their beliefs in real-time. This expression helps them explore their values and better understand the principles guiding their decisions. Articulating these beliefs not only strengthens self-confidence but also offers insights into areas where they may want to develop or adjust. Scientologists view this process of clarification as essential to personal growth, as it allows individuals to act with intentionality and integrity.

Effective communication also involves a **feedback loop** with others, which fosters self-awareness by providing external perspectives. Constructive feedback helps individuals see themselves from a different vantage point, illuminating aspects of their personality, strengths, and areas for improvement. Receiving feedback, whether about tone, body language, or communication style, allows individuals to refine their approach and align their self-image with how they are perceived. In Scientology, feedback is valued as a tool for personal growth, as it encourages individuals to engage in continuous self-assessment and improvement.

Through these communication practices, Scientologists find that **self-awareness becomes an ongoing, active process**. By engaging in honest, reflective dialogue with others, individuals continuously refine their understanding of themselves. Each conversation becomes a stepping stone for personal insight, allowing people to recognize and reshape habits, assumptions, and beliefs. This process of self-exploration through communication is seen as integral to achieving mental clarity and spiritual growth within Scientology, as it brings individuals closer to an authentic understanding of themselves and their place in the world.

## Handling Miscommunication and Conflict

Effective communication is essential for **preventing and resolving conflicts** that arise from misunderstandings or miscommunication. Miscommunication can lead to assumptions, emotional reactions, and frustration, so Scientologists are trained in techniques to recognize and address these issues proactively. Handling conflict constructively involves listening carefully, acknowledging each person's perspective, and clarifying intentions to resolve issues respectfully. Scientologists believe that by mastering these techniques, individuals can prevent small misunderstandings from escalating into major conflicts.

One primary technique for addressing miscommunication is **asking clarifying questions**. Rather than assuming the meaning behind someone's words, individuals are encouraged to ask questions that seek additional details or confirm understanding. Clarifying questions, such as "Can you explain what you meant by that?" or "Could you give me an example?" are designed to eliminate ambiguity and ensure that both parties are on the same page. Scientologists see this technique as a way to prevent misunderstandings and keep communication clear and focused, reducing the likelihood of conflict arising from misinterpretation.

When miscommunication does occur, Scientologists emphasize the importance of **taking responsibility for one's role** in the misunderstanding. Acknowledging any contribution to the confusion fosters an atmosphere of mutual respect and accountability. By saying, "I realize I may not have been clear," or "Let me rephrase that to avoid confusion," individuals demonstrate a willingness to clarify their intentions and ensure the other person's understanding. This approach encourages both parties to remain open to correction and reinforces the shared responsibility for maintaining effective communication.

During conflicts, Scientologists are trained to **stay calm and avoid reactive language**. Emotional responses, particularly anger or defensiveness, can escalate a situation quickly. Practicing techniques like deep breathing, pausing before responding, and maintaining a neutral tone can help individuals control their own reactions, keeping the conversation productive and solution-oriented. Scientologists view this approach as essential, as it allows them to focus on resolving the issue rather than becoming entangled in emotional responses. Staying calm also encourages the other person to adopt a similar tone, promoting a more constructive interaction.

In cases where conflict arises due to **differing perspectives**, Scientologists are encouraged to use active listening and acknowledgment to show understanding. Acknowledgment, such as saying, "I understand where you're coming from," or "I can see how that might be frustrating," conveys empathy and lets the other person know that their feelings are valid. This approach creates a foundation of respect, making it easier for both parties to explore solutions together. Acknowledging the other's perspective doesn't necessarily mean agreement but shows a willingness to consider their viewpoint, which is often enough to defuse tension.

To move toward resolution, Scientologists use a technique called **finding common ground**. This involves identifying areas of agreement or shared interests within the disagreement. By focusing on what they have in common, both parties can shift the conversation from confrontation to collaboration. For instance, in a disagreement about project timelines, they might agree that both want the best possible outcome and can discuss alternative approaches. Finding common ground helps bridge the gap between differing views, enabling both sides to work together toward a solution.

Another key technique for resolving conflicts in Scientology is the **use of constructive feedback**. When providing feedback, Scientologists focus on specific behaviors rather than personal judgments, keeping the feedback objective and actionable. For example, instead of saying, "You always ignore deadlines," a more constructive approach would be, "I noticed the deadline was missed, and I'd like to discuss how we can manage it more effectively in the future." This type of feedback helps prevent defensiveness and keeps the conversation focused on solutions, making it easier for both parties to work through issues.

Scientologists also use **apology and amends** as a means of conflict resolution when necessary. Taking accountability by apologizing shows respect and humility, which can be instrumental in rebuilding trust. Offering amends, such as suggesting a way to make up for an error, demonstrates a commitment to restoring harmony. This approach is seen as valuable because it not only resolves the immediate issue but also strengthens the relationship by affirming both parties' dedication to positive, ethical interactions.

# CHAPTER 13: THE SCIENTOLOGY VIEW ON LIFE AND THE UNIVERSE

## Understanding Life from a Scientology Perspective

In Scientology, **life is viewed as a dynamic and interconnected journey** that transcends physical existence. Scientologists believe that each person is a spiritual being, called a "thetan," who exists independently of the physical body and mind. This thetan is seen as the true self, possessing its own consciousness, experiences, and identity beyond the physical world. From a Scientology perspective, life isn't confined to a single lifetime; instead, it is an ongoing series of experiences that the thetan accumulates over many lifetimes. This continuity means that each individual carries knowledge, decisions, and actions from previous existences into the present, influencing their current life path and choices.

The concept of **survival** is fundamental in Scientology's view of life. Scientologists see life as driven by a central goal: the urge to survive across eight "dynamics," which are areas or dimensions of life that encompass different aspects of existence. The First Dynamic is the self, while the other dynamics expand outward to include family, groups, humankind, and ultimately all forms of life and the universe itself. Scientologists believe that achieving balance across these eight dynamics leads to a fulfilling life. Survival isn't merely about physical existence; it's about thriving, expanding one's potential, and improving conditions for oneself and others across all dynamics.

Scientologists also believe that **each individual has a purpose** unique to their spiritual journey, contributing to their own survival and the survival of others. This purpose goes beyond material goals or individual achievements; it encompasses spiritual growth, self-discovery, and helping others realize their potential. Through auditing and training, Scientologists work to uncover their individual purposes and align their actions with this deeper calling. Living in harmony with this purpose is seen as essential for spiritual fulfillment and for progressing on the Bridge to Total Freedom, the pathway within Scientology that leads to spiritual enlightenment.

Another key aspect of Scientology's view on life is the **importance of ethical conduct**. Scientologists believe that life is guided by principles of right and wrong, which contribute to the overall quality and effectiveness of one's survival. Ethical actions are those that promote well-being and align with the individual's values across the eight dynamics. Unethical actions, in contrast, are seen as destructive, leading to harm or setbacks across these areas. Maintaining personal integrity and responsibility are essential in this philosophy, as each action is believed to have a ripple effect, influencing both the individual and the broader environment.

Scientology's **view on life also encompasses a strong emphasis on self-improvement**. The philosophy encourages individuals to confront and resolve areas of mental and spiritual difficulty, such as past traumas or irrational fears, which are believed to hinder one's potential. By addressing these barriers, individuals gain greater clarity and self-awareness, enabling them to make choices that align with their true purpose. This process of self-improvement is continuous, as Scientologists believe there is always room for growth and new insights. Through auditing, they work to free themselves from past negative influences, enhancing their ability to make conscious, rational decisions.

In Scientology, life is not limited to the **material world**. Scientologists hold that the physical universe is only one aspect of existence, with the spiritual realm being equally, if not more, significant. This view means that Scientologists seek to balance their physical lives with spiritual practices that help them connect with their thetan. They believe that understanding the spiritual dimension of life offers a fuller, richer experience, enabling them to live with purpose, insight, and compassion. By recognizing the thetan as the true self, Scientologists view life as a journey toward spiritual enlightenment, transcending the limitations of the physical body and mind.

Life from a Scientology perspective is also **marked by a continuous quest for knowledge and understanding**. Scientologists see life as a learning process, where each experience offers a lesson and contributes to one's spiritual development. This search for understanding isn't limited to formal study; it includes real-world experiences, challenges, and personal interactions. Scientologists believe that through understanding themselves and the world around them, they gain the wisdom to navigate life's complexities and make decisions that promote their spiritual growth.

Scientology places significant emphasis on the concept of **personal responsibility**. Scientologists believe that individuals are accountable for their actions and their effects on others and the environment. This sense of responsibility is seen as crucial for advancing spiritually, as taking ownership of one's choices strengthens personal integrity and ethical conduct. Scientologists are encouraged to consider the impact of their decisions on all eight dynamics, promoting actions that contribute positively to themselves and others. Responsibility isn't just about individual benefit; it's about creating a harmonious world where all beings can thrive.

Another important element of life in Scientology is the **role of relationships and community**. Scientologists are taught to value connections with others, recognizing that relationships across family, friends, groups, and humanity at large contribute to a fulfilling life. The quality of these relationships is believed to reflect the individual's own spiritual development. By fostering understanding, compassion, and ethical behavior in their interactions, Scientologists work to create supportive, positive environments that allow all parties to grow and succeed. Strong, positive relationships are seen as vital to personal happiness and as a way to support one another's spiritual journeys.

Finally, Scientologists view life as **an interconnected system** where every being and element of existence has a role. The belief in interconnectedness means that actions taken by one person have effects that ripple outward, influencing others and even larger aspects of the universe. By recognizing this interconnected nature, Scientologists are motivated to act responsibly, with the understanding that their contributions, however small, shape the larger world. This view fosters a sense of unity and respect for all forms of life, encouraging Scientologists to align their lives with actions that benefit both the individual and the collective.

## The Concept of Immortality and Eternal Life

Immortality is viewed as an inherent quality of the thetan, the spiritual being that is considered each person's true self. Scientologists believe that the thetan is timeless and eternal, existing independently of the physical body or the mind. This concept of immortality is not bound to a single life but rather extends across countless lifetimes. According to Scientology, each lifetime is merely one chapter in the thetan's ongoing journey, a journey that continues through death and into new physical forms. The thetan, therefore, is believed to experience numerous incarnations, carrying knowledge, experiences, and wisdom from one existence to the next.

Scientologists hold that the **thetan's immortality gives each person infinite potential**. Because the thetan is not confined to a single body or identity, it possesses an expansive capacity for growth, learning, and self-realization. Scientology teaches that by understanding and embracing one's spiritual nature, individuals can tap into this potential, discovering aspects of themselves that go beyond physical and mental limits. This perspective fosters a sense of purpose, as each lifetime offers new opportunities to expand one's understanding and progress spiritually.

This **continuity of existence across lifetimes** shapes how Scientologists approach life and personal development. In their view, experiences and actions in one life can influence future incarnations, carrying forward any unresolved issues or unrealized potentials. Scientology's practices, like auditing and training, are therefore seen as essential for freeing the thetan from past traumas and limitations that may have accumulated across lifetimes. By addressing these barriers, Scientologists believe they can move closer to realizing their true potential and entering future lifetimes with a greater sense of clarity and purpose.

The concept of **eternal life in Scientology goes beyond individual immortality**; it connects to the larger aim of advancing spiritually toward freedom. Scientologists believe that the state of immortality isn't merely a continuation of existence but a journey toward ultimate liberation. The goal is to achieve what Scientology terms "total freedom," where the thetan is free from the constraints of the physical universe and the reactive mind. This state of total freedom represents a level of spiritual awareness and understanding that allows the thetan to exist fully as an autonomous spiritual being, unhindered by material limitations.

Immortality also implies **a broader responsibility** across lifetimes. Since Scientologists believe that actions in this life impact future incarnations, they strive to live ethically, make conscious decisions, and avoid actions that would create harmful consequences. This sense of responsibility influences the approach to ethical behavior, relationships, and personal growth. By acting in ways that align with their values and understanding, Scientologists see themselves as contributing positively to their spiritual journey and preparing for more fulfilling lives ahead.

Scientology also teaches that **achieving immortality requires continuous personal advancement**. While the thetan is naturally immortal, true spiritual freedom and awareness are seen as conditions that require active pursuit. Through auditing, training, and ethical living, Scientologists work to remove the mental and spiritual obstacles that might hinder their progress. Each step on the Bridge to Total Freedom is seen as a pathway to deeper self-knowledge and a greater alignment with the thetan's eternal nature, gradually allowing the individual to access higher levels of awareness and autonomy.

**Understanding death** is also part of Scientology's approach to immortality. Scientologists view death not as an end but as a transition, a point where the thetan leaves one body and prepares to take on another. This perspective on death alleviates fear and encourages a calm acceptance of life's cycles. Rather than fearing the unknown, Scientologists see death as a natural part of the thetan's journey, one that allows for continued spiritual evolution. This understanding fosters a sense of peace and continuity, as Scientologists believe that their experiences, insights, and spiritual growth are preserved by the thetan across each life.

In this view of eternal life, Scientology encourages its followers to **live in alignment with their spiritual goals**. Since life is continuous, each lifetime is an opportunity to advance, address unresolved matters, and approach the state of total freedom. Scientologists see each day, decision, and relationship as a meaningful part of this larger journey, using this awareness to make choices that reflect their aspirations for spiritual growth. This focus on purpose and progression influences the way Scientologists approach their personal and spiritual development, instilling a lifelong commitment to self-improvement and ethical living.

## Scientology's View of the Universe and Spiritual Realms

Scientology views the **universe as a complex, multidimensional space** that encompasses both the physical and spiritual realms. From this perspective, the physical universe—composed of matter, energy, space, and time—is just one aspect of existence. Scientologists believe that the spiritual realm, where the thetan primarily exists, transcends these physical boundaries. The thetan, as a spiritual being, is not limited by the physical universe; instead, it has the capacity to observe, influence, and exist beyond the confines of the material world. This understanding shapes Scientologists' approach to life, as they see their existence as spanning far beyond the physical reality they currently inhabit.

In Scientology, the **spiritual realm is considered a true reality** where the thetan's consciousness operates freely. This spiritual dimension is believed to be the source of one's creative power, awareness, and purpose. The physical world, while significant, is seen as temporary and subject to limitations, whereas the spiritual realm is eternal and boundless. Scientologists regard spiritual awareness as the key to navigating both realms, as a heightened understanding of the spiritual domain allows the thetan to experience greater control and freedom over their physical life. Through the practices of Scientology, such as auditing and training, individuals aim to gain insight into this realm and develop abilities that extend beyond physical constraints.

Scientologists also believe that the **universe itself is interconnected**, with each thetan having a role in its continuous creation and change. This interconnectedness suggests that every thought, action, and intention influences the universe and others within it. This view encourages Scientologists to approach life with a sense of unity and responsibility, understanding that their actions have a ripple effect throughout the cosmos. In this sense, Scientology promotes an awareness of the individual's place within a larger cosmic structure, fostering a sense of interconnected purpose.

The concept of **spiritual freedom** is central to Scientology's view of the universe. Scientologists believe that, through spiritual advancement, the thetan can eventually operate independently of the physical universe, accessing a state of true freedom. This freedom is achieved by clearing the mind of engrams and other mental barriers that tether the thetan to material limitations. Once freed, the thetan is thought to gain the ability to perceive and influence the universe in ways that transcend normal physical experience, achieving a level of awareness that Scientologists describe as total freedom.

In understanding the universe, Scientologists also acknowledge the existence of **other spiritual beings**. They believe that the universe is populated with countless thetans, each on their own journey of survival, growth, and discovery. Scientology teaches that these thetans, like oneself, are working through their own obstacles and seeking their own paths to freedom. This belief reinforces the importance of ethical interactions, empathy, and mutual respect, as each thetan's journey is interconnected with those of others.

Scientologists also consider the concept of **parallel universes or dimensions**, realms that may exist alongside the physical universe. Although these are not fully explored in early stages, Scientology's advanced teachings suggest that the thetan may have access to other levels of reality beyond the known physical plane. Scientologists believe that with sufficient spiritual advancement, the thetan can perceive and possibly influence these other dimensions, gaining deeper insights into existence and the mysteries of life.

The **structure of the universe and the thetan's place within it** are topics that Scientologists explore as they advance on the Bridge to Total Freedom. As they progress, they are encouraged to expand their awareness and understanding of how their spiritual nature interacts with the universe. This journey includes discovering their individual role and purpose within the broader existence, integrating these insights into daily life. By exploring these ideas, Scientologists aim to bridge the gap between the physical and spiritual realms, achieving a holistic view of themselves and the universe.

## Scientology's Approach to Environmental Responsibility

**Environmental responsibility is understood as an extension of the broader commitment to ethical living and survival across all eight dynamics.** These dynamics, which include the self, family, groups, humanity, and the universe itself, guide Scientologists to consider the impact of their actions on their surroundings. Scientologists believe that the environment is an interconnected aspect of the survival of all life, and they see preserving and protecting it as an ethical obligation. This view encourages Scientologists to live consciously and make decisions that support both their immediate surroundings and the larger world.

Scientology teaches that **humans, as spiritual beings (thetans), are interconnected with the environment.** This connection implies that any negative impact on the environment ultimately affects human well-being and spiritual growth. The philosophy encourages individuals to take responsibility for the quality of the environment they inhabit, as it has a direct role in physical health, mental clarity, and overall survival. Scientologists believe that a clean and healthy environment allows people to function at their best, enabling them to focus on their spiritual journey without the distraction of pollution, illness, or degradation around them.

**Personal responsibility is a central tenet of Scientology's approach to environmental care.** Scientologists are taught that each individual has a role in maintaining and improving the environment. This starts with personal actions, such as reducing waste, avoiding pollution, and making choices that contribute to environmental health. The philosophy suggests that every action, however small, has a ripple effect, and that each individual's efforts can contribute to a cleaner, more sustainable world. This personal responsibility extends to all areas of life, as Scientologists believe that responsible actions in daily life help maintain a harmonious and supportive environment for themselves and others.

**Ethical principles in Scientology emphasize the importance of reducing harm.** Scientologists believe that any behavior that damages the environment also harms humanity's chances of survival and progress. This perspective encourages Scientologists to consider the long-term effects of their actions, particularly those that could contribute to pollution, habitat destruction, or the depletion of natural resources. By evaluating their choices through an ethical lens, Scientologists aim to avoid practices that harm the environment, seeing it as an essential part of their commitment to ethical living.

In addition to personal actions, **Scientology encourages community involvement in environmental initiatives**. Many Scientology groups engage in clean-up events, recycling programs, and awareness campaigns that promote environmental responsibility. By working together to protect and restore the environment, Scientologists strengthen their communities and create positive change. These group efforts are seen as a way to uphold the principles of the third dynamic (group survival) and the fourth dynamic (the survival of humanity), as they foster collaboration and collective responsibility for a shared environment. Scientologists believe that working together not only benefits the planet but also creates a sense of unity and purpose within the community.

The concept of **responsibility across all dynamics** also guides Scientology's approach to environmental stewardship. For example, the seventh and eighth dynamics, which encompass spiritual growth and the infinite or universal dynamic, remind Scientologists of their connection to all life. This connection inspires them to respect and protect the natural world, seeing it as part of a larger spiritual framework that encompasses both the physical and spiritual realms. Scientologists view their care for the environment as a means of honoring this interconnectedness, acknowledging that their actions today impact future generations and the overall health of the planet.

**Scientology's auditing and training practices also foster a sense of environmental responsibility** by encouraging self-awareness and mindfulness. Through these practices, Scientologists work to remove mental barriers and improve their awareness of how their actions affect others, including the environment. Increased awareness leads to more conscientious behavior, as individuals become more attuned to the needs of their surroundings and the consequences of their actions. Scientologists believe that by working to improve their own ethical standards, they naturally become more respectful and responsible toward the environment.

**Education is important in Scientology's approach to environmental care**. Scientologists are encouraged to learn about environmental issues, including pollution, resource management, and sustainable practices. Understanding these issues enables them to make informed decisions and adopt behaviors that support environmental sustainability. Scientology's emphasis on continuous learning supports this goal, as individuals are encouraged to stay informed and adapt their actions to reflect the latest knowledge and practices in environmental responsibility.

Many Scientologists apply these principles by adopting **sustainable practices in their daily lives**. This includes actions like conserving energy, reducing water usage, supporting eco-friendly businesses, and recycling. Scientologists see these choices as ways to live in alignment with their values, reinforcing their commitment to the dynamics that encompass group survival, human survival, and the health of the environment. Living sustainably is viewed as an expression of ethical responsibility, as each choice contributes to the preservation of resources and the prevention of environmental harm.

In addition to personal and community efforts, **Scientologists often participate in global initiatives aimed at promoting environmental awareness and action.** This may include collaboration with other organizations, supporting conservation projects, and engaging in environmental advocacy. By participating in these larger efforts, Scientologists contribute to a broader movement for environmental change, reinforcing their commitment to survival across all dynamics. These activities also help raise awareness among the public, encouraging others to adopt similar practices that benefit the environment.

**Scientology's concept of cause and effect further emphasizes the importance of environmental responsibility.** Scientologists believe that actions have consequences and that the impact of harmful behavior on the environment can accumulate over time. This perspective reinforces the need for proactive care, as individuals are encouraged to consider the future effects of their choices. Scientologists view environmental responsibility as part of a larger commitment to ethical living, recognizing that neglect or harm to the environment could have far-reaching consequences for future generations.

**Balance is also a key principle** in Scientology's approach to environmental responsibility. Scientologists believe that living in harmony with the environment requires a balanced approach, where resources are used wisely, waste is minimized, and efforts are made to restore and protect natural ecosystems. This balance is seen as essential for the survival of humanity and the planet. Scientologists are taught that environmental degradation and resource depletion disrupt this harmony, leading to consequences that affect all living beings. Maintaining balance through responsible actions is considered a way of contributing positively to the larger interconnected system of life.

# CHAPTER 14: SCIENTOLOGY AND PERSONAL DEVELOPMENT

## The Path to Self-Improvement and Realization

**Self-improvement and self-realization** are essential parts of the spiritual journey. Scientologists believe that each individual has an innate potential that often lies dormant due to past experiences, unresolved conflicts, and mental barriers. The path to self-improvement in Scientology involves freeing oneself from these limitations to achieve a state of clarity, understanding, and empowerment. The ultimate goal is to reach one's full potential as a thetan—an immortal spiritual being. This journey is guided by specific practices, including auditing, training, and studying key principles, all of which are aimed at unlocking the true self.

The **process of self-improvement in Scientology begins with auditing**. Auditing is a structured process that allows individuals to confront and resolve past traumas and conflicts. Scientologists believe that these negative experiences, or engrams, are stored in the reactive mind and can interfere with present-day thinking, decision-making, and well-being. Through auditing, a person is guided by an auditor to identify and address these engrams, thus "clearing" them from the mind. As these engrams are released, individuals experience greater mental clarity and emotional relief, enabling them to make choices based on the present rather than being influenced by past pain. Auditing is seen as the first significant step on the path to self-improvement, as it clears the way for deeper self-discovery.

**Self-awareness is a major focus in Scientology's approach to personal development**. Scientologists are encouraged to regularly examine their thoughts, emotions, and behaviors, gaining insight into how they interact with others and the world around them. By understanding the influence of past experiences and identifying areas for growth, individuals develop a clearer sense of who they are and what they want to achieve. This self-awareness is cultivated through both auditing and training routines (TRs), exercises that teach skills like concentration, communication, and emotional control. As self-awareness grows, individuals are better able to recognize their strengths, address weaknesses, and align their actions with their goals and values.

Another key component of self-improvement in Scientology is **setting and pursuing personal goals**. Scientology emphasizes the importance of knowing one's purpose and working consistently toward fulfilling it. Setting goals provides direction and motivation, and achieving them builds confidence and self-esteem. Scientologists are encouraged to set goals across all eight dynamics of life—from personal well-being to contributing positively to humanity and the environment. This holistic approach ensures that self-improvement isn't limited to individual success but includes making a meaningful impact on the lives of others and the world.

Scientology teaches that **personal responsibility is essential for self-realization**. Taking responsibility means recognizing that one's actions, choices, and outcomes are largely within their control. By accepting responsibility for their lives, Scientologists develop a proactive attitude, focusing on solutions rather than placing blame externally. This mindset fosters resilience and independence, as individuals learn to navigate challenges with confidence. Scientologists see responsibility as empowering, as it reinforces the idea that each person has the ability to shape their own life and destiny. Embracing personal responsibility is viewed as a critical step toward becoming a fully self-realized individual.

The concept of **ethics is deeply intertwined with self-improvement** in Scientology. Ethics in this context is not about following external rules but aligning one's actions with their personal values and the principles of Scientology. Individuals are encouraged to live ethically, make decisions that promote well-being, and avoid actions that could harm themselves or others. Maintaining ethical conduct helps Scientologists stay aligned with their true goals, ensuring that their progress toward self-realization is grounded in integrity. Ethical behavior is seen as a reflection of personal strength, as it requires individuals to act consistently with their beliefs, even in challenging situations.

As Scientologists progress on their path to self-realization, they are encouraged to **cultivate positive relationships and a supportive community**. Scientology teaches that personal development doesn't happen in isolation; it's enhanced by meaningful interactions with others. By building relationships based on trust, empathy, and respect, Scientologists create an environment that supports growth and self-discovery. Relationships provide feedback, companionship, and encouragement, all of which contribute to an individual's journey. In Scientology, creating a positive impact on others is seen as part of personal growth, as it fosters a sense of purpose and connection to the broader community.

Another dimension of self-improvement in Scientology involves **continuous learning and skill development**. Scientologists are encouraged to study, train, and expand their understanding of the principles that guide their journey. Courses and training programs offer knowledge and tools to enhance personal skills, from effective communication to conflict resolution. By continually learning, Scientologists deepen their understanding of themselves, the world, and the dynamics of human relationships. This dedication to learning is viewed as essential for self-realization, as it equips individuals to overcome challenges, adapt to changes, and engage with life fully.

The ultimate goal of self-improvement in Scientology is to **achieve a state known as Clear**, in which an individual has freed themselves from the influence of the reactive mind. In this state, Scientologists believe they can operate with full awareness and self-determination, unaffected by the unconscious reactions that once held them back. Achieving Clear is considered a significant milestone, as it allows individuals to experience life with clarity, confidence, and purpose. Beyond Clear, Scientologists continue to work on higher levels of spiritual development, known as the Operating Thetan (OT) levels, to further explore and enhance their potential.

**Self-realization in Scientology goes beyond personal satisfaction; it involves discovering one's true spiritual nature**. Through Scientology practices, individuals come to see themselves not just as physical beings but as thetans— immortal spiritual entities with the capacity for infinite growth. This recognition of the spiritual self fosters a sense of purpose that transcends material success, motivating Scientologists to pursue goals that align with their eternal journey. Self-realization is seen as a process of reconnecting with this spiritual identity, enabling individuals to live with a sense of alignment and authenticity.

Ultimately, the path to self-improvement in Scientology is **an ongoing journey**. Each step, whether through auditing, training, ethical actions, or community involvement, brings individuals closer to a fuller understanding of themselves and their purpose. Scientologists believe that as they remove obstacles, take responsibility, and live in alignment with their values, they unlock higher levels of awareness and potential. Self-improvement in Scientology isn't just about achieving personal goals but realizing the potential of the thetan, creating a life that reflects one's highest ideals, and contributing positively to the world around them. Through this continuous process, Scientologists aim to achieve a state of freedom, clarity, and self-fulfillment, experiencing life as conscious, empowered spiritual beings.

# Discovering Personal Potential and Strengths

Discovering personal potential is seen as unlocking the true abilities of the thetan, the spiritual self. Scientologists believe that everyone has innate strengths and capabilities, often buried beneath layers of doubt, past experiences, and limiting beliefs. Through structured practices like auditing and training, individuals can uncover these latent abilities, bringing them to the surface. This process is designed to help each person identify and develop qualities that contribute to a life filled with purpose and effectiveness. By tapping into these strengths, Scientologists feel empowered to pursue goals that align with their deeper potential.

**Auditing** is a key practice for uncovering personal strengths in Scientology. This process involves a guided examination of past experiences, enabling individuals to confront and release mental barriers that cloud their self-awareness. Through auditing, Scientologists believe they gain insight into patterns, behaviors, and untapped skills that may have been hidden due to past conditioning or traumas. For example, someone might uncover resilience, empathy, or an ability to remain calm under pressure. As these qualities come to light, individuals are able to see themselves more clearly, recognizing strengths that had been overshadowed by doubts or insecurities.

Scientology also emphasizes **the importance of setting goals** as a way to bring out personal potential. Scientologists are encouraged to set specific, meaningful objectives that require them to stretch their abilities and take on new challenges. By pursuing goals across different areas of life—whether personal, professional, or spiritual—individuals push themselves beyond their comfort zones, developing qualities like perseverance, creativity, and focus. Setting and achieving goals builds confidence, reinforcing the belief that each person has the power to shape their own path. This practice of setting and reaching goals helps individuals understand and expand their capabilities over time.

The **training routines (TRs)** practiced in Scientology also contribute to discovering personal strengths. These routines are exercises designed to improve focus, emotional control, and communication. Through TRs, Scientologists learn to observe their own reactions and maintain calmness and composure, even in challenging situations. This self-discipline helps reveal inner strengths, as individuals learn to handle distractions, manage emotions, and communicate effectively. Over time, the mastery of these skills builds a strong foundation of self-assurance and clarity, allowing Scientologists to navigate their lives with purpose and confidence.

Scientology encourages individuals to **reflect on their accomplishments and recognize their strengths** as a means of developing self-belief. By taking the time to acknowledge what they've achieved and identify the qualities that helped them succeed, Scientologists reinforce a positive self-image. This reflection helps them understand how their abilities contribute to their overall goals, encouraging further growth. Scientologists see this self-recognition as crucial, as it allows individuals to approach future challenges with greater confidence in their strengths and potential.

The concept of **eight dynamics** in Scientology also supports the exploration of personal potential. These dynamics, which represent different aspects of life—from self to family, groups, humankind, and beyond—serve as a framework for evaluating and developing one's strengths. Scientologists work to cultivate qualities that benefit each dynamic, fostering a balanced approach to growth. This perspective encourages individuals to develop qualities that not only enhance their personal lives but also contribute to the well-being of others and the environment. Through this holistic approach, individuals discover the strengths that allow them to thrive in all aspects of life.

**Continuous learning and skill development** are central to the process of realizing personal potential in Scientology. Scientologists are encouraged to study, train, and seek knowledge that will support their personal and spiritual goals. By acquiring new skills and expanding their understanding of themselves and the world, they can unlock higher levels of potential. This commitment to lifelong learning reflects the belief that each person has a limitless capacity for growth and improvement. In this way, discovering personal potential becomes an ongoing process, with each new skill or insight bringing individuals closer to their fullest expression.

# Overcoming Negative Influences and Behaviors

Overcoming negative influences is essential to self-improvement. Scientologists believe that **negative influences often stem from unresolved past experiences** and can create mental or emotional obstacles that hinder personal growth. Through auditing, individuals confront these negative experiences directly, freeing themselves from their hold. Scientologists consider this process vital because it clears the mind of harmful influences, allowing individuals to act with more clarity and intention. By resolving these influences, they are better equipped to handle life's challenges and pursue their goals without being limited by past setbacks.

Negative behaviors, or **reactive patterns**, are also addressed through Scientology's personal development practices. Reactive patterns are automatic responses to certain triggers that Scientologists believe come from the reactive mind. These patterns might include anger, self-doubt, or procrastination, which can disrupt progress and reduce personal effectiveness. Through auditing, Scientologists identify these patterns and work to release the underlying engrams—mental images associated with pain or loss—that fuel them. The goal is to reach a state where the reactive mind no longer controls behavior, allowing for a more conscious and deliberate approach to life.

**Ethical living** is another cornerstone of overcoming negative influences in Scientology. Scientologists are encouraged to examine their behavior and take responsibility for their actions, identifying any habits or behaviors that don't align with their values or goals. By cultivating a strong ethical foundation, individuals create a mindset that resists negative influences, as ethical behavior reinforces a sense of self-discipline and integrity. When individuals act in accordance with their principles, they strengthen their resolve to make choices that benefit themselves and others, effectively minimizing the impact of harmful behaviors.

Scientologists also use **specific techniques to handle external negative influences**. These influences may come from toxic relationships, stressful environments, or negative social interactions. Scientology teaches methods for handling and, if necessary, disengaging from influences that cause harm or hold a person back. By learning to set boundaries, individuals protect themselves from being affected by negative external forces. This focus on managing external influences is based on the understanding that while some aspects of life are outside one's control, individuals have the power to control their responses and protect their well-being.

**Communication training** further supports the ability to overcome negative behaviors. Through training routines, Scientologists practice handling criticism, difficult conversations, and emotionally charged situations with calmness and poise. These routines help them avoid reactive responses, allowing them to engage constructively without letting negative emotions drive their actions. Communication training also builds resilience, as it teaches individuals how to maintain their composure even in challenging interactions. This skillset is valuable for navigating everyday situations that might otherwise trigger negative behaviors.

**Self-assessment and reflection** are key in overcoming negative behaviors. Scientologists are taught to regularly examine their thoughts, actions, and motivations, identifying any behaviors or tendencies that hinder their progress. By reflecting on their choices, they gain a deeper understanding of what drives them and learn to adjust their actions accordingly. This process of self-assessment promotes continuous improvement, as individuals are able to make conscious decisions that support their goals and values. The practice of self-reflection also strengthens personal accountability, as individuals become more mindful of their actions and their impact.

For Scientologists, **handling conflict and stress** effectively is also part of overcoming negative behaviors. Stressful situations often trigger automatic responses, but Scientology teaches techniques to manage these moments with awareness. Individuals learn to approach conflicts constructively, finding solutions rather than reacting impulsively. By developing the skills to handle stress and conflict, Scientologists gain control over their emotions, avoiding the negative responses that can arise in difficult situations. This approach empowers them to maintain focus on their goals, even in the face of external challenges.

Through these practices, Scientologists work to **replace negative behaviors with constructive actions**, transforming reactions into conscious choices. This transformation supports long-term growth and aligns individuals with their values, enabling them to pursue a life that reflects their true potential. By overcoming negative influences and behaviors, Scientologists believe they can experience life with greater freedom, effectiveness, and clarity, fully engaging in their journey of self-discovery and personal development.

## Building Emotional Resilience

**Emotional resilience** is regarded as an essential quality for personal growth and spiritual advancement. Scientologists believe that resilience allows individuals to navigate life's challenges with strength and composure, minimizing the impact of negative emotions and setbacks. By building resilience, they become better equipped to handle the ups and downs of life while maintaining focus on their goals and well-being. Emotional resilience in Scientology is cultivated through practices such as auditing, communication training, and regular self-reflection, all of which aim to strengthen the mind and spirit.

**Auditing is a key activity** for developing emotional resilience, as it helps individuals confront and release past traumas, painful memories, and unresolved conflicts. These emotional burdens, known as engrams, are stored in the reactive mind and can trigger automatic responses that disrupt mental clarity and balance.

Through auditing sessions, Scientologists work to clear these engrams, which they believe can free them from emotional reactivity. With each layer of negative experiences addressed, individuals feel more emotionally stable and less prone to being influenced by past hurts. This sense of clarity allows them to approach new situations with a calm and composed mind.

**Training Routines (TRs)** also contribute significantly to emotional resilience by enhancing a person's ability to remain present, focused, and in control during interactions. TRs teach Scientologists to stay grounded even in challenging situations, such as conversations where they might face criticism, distractions, or conflicting viewpoints. For example, TR 0—where participants practice sitting face-to-face with another person without reacting—trains them to observe their own impulses and remain calm under pressure. This ability to maintain emotional control strengthens their resilience, as they learn to handle difficult moments without being thrown off balance.

**Self-awareness is another cornerstone of emotional resilience** in Scientology. Regularly examining one's own thoughts, emotions, and reactions helps individuals understand how they respond to stress, criticism, or conflict. This self-awareness enables them to identify emotional patterns, such as anger or fear, and take proactive steps to manage these responses. Through self-reflection and auditing, Scientologists can observe how past experiences have influenced their emotional reactions and gain insight into how to prevent these patterns from reoccurring. This self-knowledge allows them to face challenges with greater confidence, aware of their strengths and potential vulnerabilities.

In Scientology, **empathy and understanding** are seen as important for developing emotional resilience. Scientologists learn to view interactions from multiple perspectives, which reduces emotional conflicts and fosters a calm, understanding approach to disagreements. By practicing empathy, they can see situations objectively rather than reactively, allowing them to engage without feeling defensive or threatened. This empathic approach helps Scientologists handle emotionally charged situations with poise, understanding that each person has their own unique experiences and perspectives.

**Regular communication drills and practical exercises** further build resilience by strengthening skills like patience, focus, and conflict resolution. By practicing constructive communication, individuals learn to express their feelings calmly and assertively without letting negative emotions control their actions. These exercises teach Scientologists to respond thoughtfully in difficult conversations, remaining resilient against emotional triggers. This focus on effective communication fosters resilience not only by reinforcing self-control but by teaching individuals to resolve conflicts and misunderstandings in a calm and respectful way.

In addition, **developing strong ethical standards** supports emotional resilience in Scientology. Scientologists believe that acting in alignment with one's values fosters a stable sense of self, reducing the likelihood of inner conflict or regret. When individuals make choices based on their ethical beliefs, they feel grounded in their decisions, which provides a foundation for emotional resilience. Adhering to personal integrity enables Scientologists to face challenges with confidence, as they know they are acting consistently with their principles. This consistency in action supports emotional stability, especially during times of stress or adversity.

For Scientologists, building emotional resilience is an ongoing process, strengthened through regular practice and reflection. By combining these techniques—auditing, training routines, ethical living, and self-awareness—individuals gradually enhance their ability to face challenges with calmness, clarity, and resolve. Emotional resilience allows Scientologists to remain true to their path of personal development, steadily progressing even in the face of life's uncertainties.

## Developing Discipline and Consistency in Practice

In Scientology, **discipline and consistency** are seen as vital for achieving personal and spiritual growth. The journey of self-improvement, according to Scientology, requires a committed approach, as each step forward builds on the last. Scientologists practice discipline by engaging regularly in activities like auditing, studying Scientology materials, and applying what they've learned in daily life. Developing discipline allows individuals to persist through challenges and stay focused on their goals, which reinforces steady progress on the Bridge to Total Freedom.

**Auditing requires a disciplined approach** to be effective. Scientologists are encouraged to attend regular auditing sessions, working consistently through layers of past experiences and mental barriers. This regular practice ensures that they stay on track with their spiritual progress. Because auditing sessions build upon one another, consistency is essential for reaching deeper levels of self-awareness. Each session contributes to a gradual release of engrams, helping Scientologists uncover new insights and free themselves from past limitations. By maintaining a steady auditing schedule, they strengthen their commitment to personal growth and create momentum on their path of self-discovery.

**Studying Scientology materials** is another practice that emphasizes discipline. Scientologists are encouraged to read and study materials written by L. Ron Hubbard, which outline the principles of Scientology and provide guidance on applying these teachings. Consistent study helps individuals internalize these concepts, enabling them to apply them in their lives more effectively. This ongoing learning process reinforces the importance of staying disciplined, as Scientologists are reminded of the principles they are working to embody. Through disciplined study, they gain a deeper understanding of Scientology's philosophy, which strengthens their resolve to live according to its teachings.

Scientologists also engage in **Training Routines (TRs) regularly** to improve communication and focus. These exercises require patience, concentration, and a steady commitment to practice. By performing TRs consistently, Scientologists develop self-control and the ability to stay present, even in challenging situations. Discipline in practicing TRs is seen as essential, as each repetition refines a skill needed for effective communication and interaction. With ongoing practice, individuals become better equipped to handle distractions, stay focused on their goals, and interact with others constructively, all of which are important qualities for personal and spiritual growth.

**Adhering to ethical guidelines** is another aspect of discipline in Scientology. Scientologists are encouraged to align their actions with their values, maintaining a consistent ethical standard. This requires self-discipline, as they strive to avoid behaviors that might disrupt their progress or create inner conflict. By acting in accordance with their beliefs and maintaining ethical consistency, Scientologists strengthen their commitment to their spiritual path. This approach supports emotional stability, resilience, and a focused mindset, as individuals build trust in their ability to make choices that reflect their values.

**Time management** is also emphasized as part of maintaining consistency in practice. Scientologists are taught to manage their time wisely, balancing their personal development with responsibilities to family, work, and community. Setting aside time for auditing, study, and training routines requires planning and commitment, reinforcing the importance of prioritizing one's spiritual goals. By managing their time effectively, Scientologists demonstrate their dedication to self-improvement, ensuring that they have the resources and focus needed to progress steadily. Time management supports consistency, as individuals are able to engage in practices regularly without neglecting other areas of their lives.

**Overcoming distractions and staying focused** are also part of developing discipline. Scientologists learn techniques to handle distractions, whether internal (such as self-doubt or impatience) or external (such as social obligations or work pressures). By practicing techniques to maintain focus, individuals become adept at staying on track with their goals, even when faced with obstacles. This ability to stay disciplined amidst distractions reinforces their commitment to growth, allowing them to make meaningful progress without being sidetracked.

For Scientologists, discipline and consistency are not simply about routine; they are about creating a solid foundation for continued spiritual progress. Through regular practice, disciplined study, and ethical consistency, Scientologists build the skills and mindset necessary to reach higher levels of self-awareness and personal fulfillment. This dedication to discipline ensures that they remain aligned with their spiritual goals, steadily advancing toward the freedom and clarity they seek.

# CHAPTER 15: SCIENTOLOGY IN SOCIETY

## Scientology's Social Programs and Initiatives

**Social programs and initiatives** reflect a commitment to improving conditions for individuals and communities worldwide. These programs, inspired by L. Ron Hubbard's teachings, aim to address social issues by providing practical tools and resources. From education and literacy programs to drug prevention and rehabilitation, Scientology's outreach efforts are designed to help people build better lives. By creating initiatives that target the root causes of social challenges, Scientologists believe they can make a lasting impact on society.

One of Scientology's most prominent social programs is **The Truth About Drugs campaign**, which focuses on drug education and prevention. Scientologists believe that substance abuse is a major barrier to personal growth and well-being, affecting families, communities, and societies as a whole. The Truth About Drugs campaign provides factual information about the effects of drugs on the mind and body, aiming to prevent drug use before it starts. This campaign includes educational materials, seminars, and partnerships with schools and community groups, offering information that young people can use to make informed choices. Scientologists see this initiative as a proactive approach to reducing substance abuse and its impact on society.

**Narconon** is another significant program associated with Scientology, aimed at helping individuals overcome drug and alcohol addiction. This drug rehabilitation program is based on Hubbard's principles, focusing on a holistic approach that addresses both the physical and mental aspects of addiction. Narconon combines detoxification techniques with life skills training, aiming to support individuals in reclaiming control over their lives. By providing non-medical rehabilitation services, Narconon seeks to help individuals achieve lasting recovery without relying on substitute drugs. Scientologists view Narconon as a way to offer meaningful support to those affected by addiction, helping them build a foundation for a drug-free life.

In the field of **human rights advocacy**, Scientology's United for Human Rights campaign promotes awareness of basic human rights as outlined in the Universal Declaration of Human Rights. Scientologists believe that understanding and respecting human rights are essential for building a just and equitable society. Through educational materials, public events, and partnerships with organizations, United for Human Rights works to inform people about their rights and inspire them to take action. This program also includes a youth-focused component, Youth for Human Rights International, which educates young people about human rights principles through videos, booklets, and interactive activities. Scientologists see this advocacy work as a step toward a world where individual freedoms are protected and upheld.

**The Way to Happiness** campaign is another initiative that seeks to promote moral values and ethical living in communities. This campaign is based on *The Way to Happiness*, a booklet written by Hubbard that outlines 21 common-sense precepts for living a fulfilling and ethical life. The campaign distributes millions of copies of the booklet worldwide, reaching people in schools, prisons, community centers, and more. The Way to Happiness emphasizes principles like respect, honesty, and responsibility, providing a guide for personal conduct that Scientologists believe can foster greater harmony and understanding within society. By promoting these values, the campaign aims to improve the moral fabric of communities, reducing conflict and promoting positive behavior.

**Scientology Volunteer Ministers** provide disaster relief and community support in areas affected by crises. The Volunteer Ministers program trains individuals to assist in emergencies, offering help in natural disasters, conflict zones, and other challenging environments. Volunteers provide practical aid, such as food and shelter, while also offering Scientology-based techniques to help people cope with trauma and stress. Scientologists see Volunteer Ministers as a way to offer immediate assistance and emotional support, helping communities recover and rebuild. The program has responded to disasters worldwide, from earthquakes and hurricanes to pandemics, reflecting Scientology's commitment to humanitarian aid.

In addition to these programs, **literacy and education** initiatives supported by Scientology address barriers to learning, especially in underprivileged communities. Through programs like Applied Scholastics, Scientologists provide training in Hubbard's Study Technology, which emphasizes methods to help students understand and retain information more effectively. Study Technology aims to improve comprehension by addressing barriers to learning, such as misunderstood words or lack of interest. By equipping educators, parents, and students with these tools, Scientologists believe they can improve literacy rates and foster a love for learning. Applied Scholastics works with schools and organizations globally, offering workshops, materials, and teacher training programs that support effective education.

Through these social programs, Scientologists aim to address various challenges and improve the quality of life in communities around the world. By focusing on issues like addiction, education, human rights, and disaster relief, Scientology's initiatives seek to make practical contributions to society. Each program aligns with Scientology's belief in the importance of personal empowerment and ethical responsibility, working to create a positive impact and promote resilience across diverse populations.

## Community Outreach and Social Justice

Community outreach is considered essential for building understanding and improving conditions locally and globally. Scientologists believe that **effective change starts within communities**, and they work to bring resources and support where it is needed most. Through a range of outreach efforts, including educational programs, workshops, and events, Scientologists engage with diverse groups to address social challenges, from literacy and education to drug prevention. Community members are invited to learn practical tools and skills based on L. Ron Hubbard's teachings, enabling them to handle personal and social issues more effectively.

One of the ways Scientologists engage in social justice is by **addressing systemic issues that create inequality or hinder personal growth**. Scientology's social programs focus on providing tools that empower individuals to take control of their lives, regardless of their background. Scientologists believe that by addressing issues like substance abuse, illiteracy, and lack of basic education, they can reduce the factors that contribute to social injustice. Through the Truth About Drugs program, for instance, they educate youth and community members on the effects of drugs, equipping them to make informed choices and avoid substance-related challenges.

**Youth outreach is also central to Scientology's social justice initiatives**. Programs like Youth for Human Rights work within schools and communities to inform young people about their fundamental rights and responsibilities. By promoting awareness of human rights, Scientologists aim to inspire the next generation to advocate for equality, respect, and compassion. This focus on education and empowerment is designed to address injustices at the root, fostering a generation that is better equipped to create positive change in their communities.

Through volunteer work and outreach programs, Scientologists aim to **strengthen social bonds and promote ethical living**. Volunteer Ministers, for example, work with communities to offer practical assistance in times of need, from disaster relief to conflict zones. Scientologists believe that by being present in communities, offering support and ethical guidance, they can help build safer, more resilient societies. These community efforts embody Scientology's commitment to supporting social justice, empowering individuals to overcome obstacles and live with dignity and purpose.

## Scientology's View on World Peace and Coexistence

Scientology holds that **world peace and coexistence are achievable when individuals live ethically and embrace mutual understanding**. Scientologists believe that peace begins with the individual, as each person's actions and mindset contribute to the state of the larger world. The philosophy of Scientology emphasizes personal responsibility, ethical conduct, and a commitment to creating harmony with others. By promoting these values, Scientologists aim to foster an environment where peace and coexistence are possible, both on an individual and a societal level.

The foundation for world peace in Scientology lies in **respect for the rights and freedoms of others**. Scientologists are taught to value and protect individual rights as essential for creating a stable and peaceful society. Programs like United for Human Rights and Youth for Human Rights International educate people on the Universal Declaration of Human Rights, encouraging respect and understanding between diverse communities. Scientologists believe that, by raising awareness of these fundamental rights, individuals and groups can address conflicts constructively, reducing the potential for violence or oppression.

Scientology's concept of **eight dynamics** also supports coexistence by recognizing the importance of survival across all areas of life, from the self to humanity and beyond. Scientologists strive to live harmoniously within these dynamics, understanding that survival is not limited to individual goals but includes the welfare of families, communities, and nations. By considering the survival needs of all these levels, they promote coexistence that balances individual freedoms with social responsibility. This interconnected approach fosters an appreciation for the well-being of others, seeing humanity's future as a shared responsibility.

Through **educational initiatives and outreach programs**, Scientologists work to encourage a spirit of peace and cooperation. They believe that providing people with tools to improve their lives helps reduce social tensions and conflicts, creating an environment where peaceful coexistence is possible. For instance, programs that address literacy, drug prevention, and ethical conduct are seen as ways to remove barriers to understanding and cooperation. By helping people achieve personal stability and empowerment, Scientologists believe they can reduce sources of conflict and support a more peaceful society.

In their pursuit of world peace, Scientologists also advocate for **ethical decision-making and personal responsibility**. They believe that each person has the power to influence their surroundings, and that ethical actions build trust, reduce fear, and foster respect among individuals and nations. This emphasis on ethics aligns with their vision of a world where people coexist peacefully, based on mutual understanding and shared values. By living ethically and promoting respect, Scientologists aim to contribute to a society where differences are embraced, conflicts are minimized, and peace is possible on both local and global scales.


## Why Is Scientology So Popular in Hollywood?


Scientology has garnered significant attention in Hollywood, attracting a variety of actors, directors, producers, and other entertainment professionals over the decades. Several factors contribute to its popularity among Hollywood figures, from the promise of personal development to its unique support network. Scientology's presence in Hollywood has also been fueled by its focus on self-improvement, personal empowerment, and career success, all of which align well with the high-stakes, high-pressure environment of the entertainment industry. Here's a deeper look at why Scientology has gained traction among Hollywood celebrities and industry insiders.

One of the primary reasons **Scientology appeals to Hollywood is its emphasis on personal growth and overcoming mental barriers**. In an industry where success and failure are often measured by public perception, professional rejection, and fierce competition, Scientology offers a structured pathway to increase self-confidence and mental resilience. Through auditing, a key Scientology practice, individuals explore and release past traumas and negative experiences, known as engrams, that can create mental barriers. Many in Hollywood, where emotional resilience and clarity are essential for career longevity, find value in this process. Auditing is said to help members become more self-aware and confident, qualities that are particularly beneficial in an industry that demands constant reinvention and perseverance.

**Self-empowerment and control over one's career are also significant draws**. Scientology teaches that individuals have the power to influence their reality and achieve their goals through focused intention, a concept referred to as "postulates" within the Church. This aligns with Hollywood's culture of self-made success, where actors, directors, and other industry professionals often navigate high-stakes decisions, public scrutiny, and professional uncertainties. Scientologists believe that by gaining control over their own minds and emotions, they can more effectively direct their lives and careers. In a field where instability is common, many find Scientology's teachings on self-determination, personal responsibility, and ethical conduct reassuring.

Scientology's **community and networking opportunities** are another reason for its popularity in Hollywood. Scientology operates major centers in Los Angeles, such as the Celebrity Centre International, which caters specifically to the needs of entertainers and other high-profile members. These centers provide a supportive environment where members can meet like-minded individuals, share ideas, and build relationships. For Hollywood professionals, who often experience intense competition and isolation, belonging to a community of people who share similar goals and values can be extremely appealing. This support network extends beyond career concerns, as the Church promotes an inclusive atmosphere for handling personal, emotional, and professional challenges.

The **Celebrity Centre** itself has a unique role in Scientology's Hollywood appeal. Established to provide tailored support for artists, musicians, and other creative professionals, the Celebrity Centre offers a range of services to meet the specific needs of entertainers. This includes courses on communication, personal development, and stress management—all practical skills for individuals in high-profile professions. Additionally, the Centre is designed as a retreat where members can recharge, away from the pressures of public life. This specialized environment, exclusively designed for artists and entertainers, has become a major draw for Hollywood figures who appreciate the tailored services and the privacy it affords.

Another factor in Scientology's popularity among Hollywood figures is its **emphasis on fame and influence as a force for positive change**. Scientology promotes the idea that celebrities have a special role in society, as their public visibility allows them to reach a wide audience and set a positive example. This resonates with many Hollywood figures, who may already view their platform as an opportunity for influence. Scientologists believe that by developing spiritually and living ethically, they can serve as role models for others, embodying the principles of Scientology in their lives and careers. For those in Hollywood, this perspective reinforces the idea that their success and influence can be used to promote positive change, aligning their personal achievements with a broader purpose.

**Scientology's approach to personal privacy and security** is another appealing aspect for Hollywood professionals. Given the scrutiny that comes with fame, many celebrities are understandably concerned about protecting their private lives from media intrusion. Scientology places a high value on confidentiality within its practices, especially during auditing sessions, which involve discussions of personal and sensitive experiences. For many Hollywood figures, this promise of privacy is an attractive benefit, as it allows them to engage in self-exploration without fear of public exposure. The Church also offers additional protections to help members handle external pressures and media attention, giving them tools to manage their public image and personal boundaries more effectively.

Scientology's focus on **developing skills that enhance one's public and personal life** aligns with the needs of Hollywood professionals. For example, communication courses offered by Scientology focus on public speaking, confidence, and poise—qualities essential for success in the entertainment industry. Through training routines (TRs), Scientologists practice techniques to improve their communication skills, helping them connect more effectively with audiences, colleagues, and collaborators. In an industry where charisma and effective communication are key, these tools help Hollywood professionals refine their craft and manage interactions confidently, both on and off the screen.

The **Church's commitment to social programs and humanitarian initiatives** also resonates with Hollywood's philanthropic culture. Scientology is involved in drug education, human rights advocacy, and community outreach through programs like Narconon, United for Human Rights, and The Way to Happiness campaign. Many Hollywood figures, who are often active in charitable causes, find a natural alignment between their own values and Scientology's outreach efforts. This shared commitment to social betterment adds to Scientology's appeal, as it provides members with avenues to contribute to causes they care about, further integrating their personal beliefs with their spiritual practices.

Lastly, **Scientology's structured approach to spiritual progression** may appeal to Hollywood professionals who seek personal advancement beyond traditional religious practices. The Bridge to Total Freedom, a step-by-step path to spiritual enlightenment, offers a clear and achievable roadmap for those looking to develop themselves spiritually. This methodical approach, unique to Scientology, provides individuals with measurable milestones that mark their progress, helping them feel a sense of achievement and continuity. For those in Hollywood who often work in a results-driven environment, this tangible path toward spiritual growth can be appealing as it mirrors the professional goals they set in their careers.

In short, Scientology's popularity in Hollywood can be attributed to its practical approach to personal growth, emotional resilience, and spiritual advancement. The Church's focus on supporting the unique needs of entertainers, combined with the benefits of privacy, networking, and tailored resources, creates a strong appeal for those in high-profile professions. By addressing both the personal and professional demands of Hollywood life, Scientology has established itself as a compelling path for many seeking both success and self-realization in the public eye.

## Why Is Scientology Considered Secretive?

Scientology is widely considered secretive due to its layered structure, controlled dissemination of information, and strict confidentiality regarding its advanced teachings. Its reputation for secrecy has been fueled by multiple factors, including the way information is revealed to members only after specific levels of advancement, the confidentiality surrounding auditing sessions, and the intense privacy policies that govern its materials and internal practices. These elements contribute to the perception that Scientology is closed off to outsiders, protecting its teachings and members from scrutiny.

One of the most significant reasons Scientology is perceived as secretive is due to the **structure of its teachings**, especially the higher levels of the Bridge to Total Freedom. Scientology operates on a tiered system, where members progress through levels called Operating Thetan (OT) levels, each offering progressively more advanced spiritual knowledge. However, access to these teachings is strictly controlled. Scientologists are not permitted to view certain materials until they reach the appropriate level, and these teachings are typically not available to the public. This practice creates an aura of exclusivity around Scientology's advanced knowledge, reinforcing a sense of mystery for non-members and even for members who have yet to progress to higher levels.

**Confidentiality is a core principle** in Scientology's approach to auditing, one of its central practices. Auditing sessions, which involve a trained auditor guiding a Scientologist through past experiences to release traumas, are considered deeply private. The personal and potentially sensitive nature of these sessions contributes to the secrecy, as Scientologists are assured that their discussions remain confidential. This secrecy around auditing practices is partly protective, as many members share sensitive personal histories and psychological experiences. However, the intense confidentiality requirements surrounding auditing, including prohibiting members from discussing their experiences outside of the session, add to the perception that Scientology guards its processes closely.

Another factor contributing to the perception of secrecy is **Scientology's internal policies on confidentiality and control over information**. Scientologists are discouraged from discussing their experiences, training, and auditing outside of official church settings. Certain materials, particularly those for OT levels, are kept under strict lock and key in church locations and cannot be viewed outside. Members must sign confidentiality agreements before accessing these materials. Additionally, members may face disciplinary action for sharing internal information or practices with outsiders. This strict control over information ensures that Scientology's teachings remain proprietary and protected from outside interpretation or criticism, reinforcing its image as a closed organization.

Scientology also places a **high value on protecting intellectual property**, which is another reason why its teachings are kept private. Many of L. Ron Hubbard's writings and lectures are trademarked and copyrighted by the church, limiting how and where they can be shared. The church has taken legal actions to prevent unauthorized access or distribution of its materials, even among former members. This legal protection adds another layer of secrecy, as it prevents individuals from reproducing or publicly sharing Scientology's teachings, particularly advanced materials. This stance on intellectual property protection has created tension between Scientology and those who seek greater transparency about its practices.

**Financial requirements for access to advanced materials** also contribute to Scientology's secretive reputation. Members often pay significant fees for auditing sessions, training, and materials, especially at the higher levels of the Bridge to Total Freedom. Critics argue that this creates a barrier to entry, limiting access to information based on financial capability. This financial structure, combined with the tiered progression system, means that only committed members who can afford these fees gain access to the most advanced teachings, which are guarded closely. As a result, many people view Scientology as an organization that withholds knowledge unless members are willing to pay for it, reinforcing the perception of exclusivity and secrecy.

**The Church's intense focus on protecting its public image** also adds to its secretive reputation. Scientology has a well-known history of actively defending itself against criticism, whether from former members, media, or external organizations. The church has been known to respond to criticism with legal action or public statements countering negative portrayals. This defensive approach has led to a reputation for closely monitoring external perceptions and controlling the narrative around Scientology. Additionally, members are often discouraged from engaging with media or critics, which restricts public discussion about Scientology practices and policies. This emphasis on image control contributes to the perception that Scientology avoids transparency.

Scientology's policy of **disconnection** is another practice that fuels perceptions of secrecy. Members are sometimes encouraged or even required to cut ties with people deemed "suppressive" or harmful to their spiritual progress, which can include critics, former members, or even close family members who speak out against Scientology. This disconnection policy creates an environment where communication with outsiders is limited, further isolating members from the external world and information that may challenge their beliefs. The secrecy surrounding this policy is amplified by the fact that members are discouraged from discussing the practice openly, and the Church has downplayed or denied its use despite testimonies from former members.

**Strict internal policies and monitoring** within Scientology's ranks also contribute to its secretive image. Scientology organizations have strict codes of conduct and reporting systems, including Knowledge Reports, where members are encouraged to report ethical violations or suspicious behaviors among their peers. This internal surveillance system creates an atmosphere of vigilance, where members may be wary of sharing information or deviating from church-approved beliefs and practices. This controlled environment fosters a sense of caution among members and restricts open communication, both internally and with outsiders, which can give the impression of an organization that prioritizes secrecy over transparency.

The **Celebrity Centre** in Hollywood, a Scientology facility specifically for celebrities, is an example of how Scientology maintains distinct spaces and practices that are inaccessible to the general public. While Scientology's Celebrity Centre is a hub for actors, musicians, and other public figures, it operates with a high level of privacy. The Centre offers exclusive services tailored to the needs of entertainment professionals and maintains a culture of confidentiality around its high-profile members. This facility, along with other private centers, adds to the public perception of Scientology as a selective and secretive organization, especially given the special treatment and protected status offered to certain members.

**Scientology's Sea Organization (Sea Org)** further underscores its reputation for secrecy. The Sea Org is an elite group within Scientology that dedicates itself to full-time service, often signing a symbolic billion-year contract to serve the church for eternity. Sea Org members follow strict codes of conduct and live in a communal, structured environment where daily activities, relationships, and even leisure time are closely regulated. Due to the organization's highly regimented lifestyle and the significant commitment required from its members, outsiders have limited knowledge of the details surrounding life in the Sea Org. This insular and disciplined environment has been described by former members as highly secretive, especially regarding internal operations, member expectations, and disciplinary practices.

In addition, **Scientology's historical practices related to the "Fair Game" policy** add to its secretive image. The Fair Game policy, established in the 1960s, outlined how Scientology would handle critics or perceived enemies. Although Scientology has stated that the policy is no longer in effect, its historical use to address opposition or criticism created a legacy of secrecy and defensiveness. The policy encouraged the active handling or neutralization of critics, including legal actions and social isolation, reinforcing Scientology's reputation for protecting itself aggressively from outside scrutiny.

## Advocating for Human Rights and Equality

Scientology's commitment to human rights and equality is deeply rooted in the belief that **every person deserves respect, dignity, and the opportunity to achieve their full potential**. Through programs like United for Human Rights, Scientologists work to promote awareness of fundamental rights as outlined in the Universal Declaration of Human Rights. This initiative provides educational materials, hosts events, and collaborates with organizations to spread knowledge of human rights and inspire people to protect these freedoms. Scientologists believe that raising awareness is essential for creating a world where equality and justice are accessible to everyone.

Youth for Human Rights International, a youth-focused branch of the human rights campaign, emphasizes **educating young people about their rights**. Scientologists see youth as key to building a future that values equality and freedom. Through interactive resources, workshops, and school programs, Youth for Human Rights encourages children and teenagers to understand their rights and responsibilities. Scientologists believe that by educating youth about these principles early on, they help create a generation that values justice and actively works to uphold human rights.

Scientologists advocate for human rights as part of their **commitment to ethical behavior and social responsibility**. They believe that upholding the rights of others aligns with the principles of the eight dynamics, where each individual's survival is interconnected with the well-being of others. By fostering respect for others' rights and freedoms, Scientologists work to create communities where individuals can thrive without fear of discrimination or oppression. This advocacy for human rights is seen as an extension of their ethical framework, aiming to build a world where everyone has the opportunity to live freely and with dignity.

Scientology's outreach also extends to **supporting human rights in areas facing systemic discrimination or injustice**. Through partnerships with local organizations, Scientologists bring resources and support to communities affected by poverty, inequality, or lack of access to education. These efforts focus on empowering individuals to recognize and advocate for their rights, providing tools for self-sufficiency and resilience. Scientologists believe that by addressing barriers to equality, they help communities achieve stability and independence, paving the way for a more just society.

Scientologists see **human rights advocacy as a way to bridge cultural, social, and political divides**. By promoting universal rights that transcend individual differences, they encourage understanding and unity among diverse populations.

# CHAPTER 16: THE FUTURE OF SCIENTOLOGY

## The Vision of a Clear Planet

In Scientology, the **vision of a Clear Planet** reflects the ultimate goal of creating a world where individuals are free from the influence of the reactive mind and can live with clarity, purpose, and ethical integrity. This vision is rooted in the concept of a "Clear" individual—someone who has overcome the mental barriers of engrams, those stored memories of past traumas that cloud perception and limit personal growth. In Scientology, achieving the state of Clear allows individuals to experience life fully, making choices without interference from subconscious reactions. Extending this vision to a planetary level, a Clear Planet would be a society where people worldwide have reached this state, transforming humanity's collective behavior and potential.

The **Bridge to Total Freedom** is central to this vision. Scientologists see the Bridge as a path to spiritual enlightenment that allows individuals to progress from a state of pre-Clear to Clear, and ultimately, to the higher levels of spiritual awareness known as the Operating Thetan (OT) levels. By helping more people move up this Bridge, Scientologists believe they can reduce conflict, increase understanding, and foster a society that values compassion, responsibility, and freedom. A Clear Planet would be one where the majority of people have experienced the benefits of auditing, which clears the mind of negative influences and enhances awareness, leaving individuals better equipped to contribute positively to society.

Scientologists envision a Clear Planet as a world without the **barriers of unconscious reactions** and unresolved traumas. In their view, much of human conflict and suffering comes from these hidden mental influences, which lead to irrational behaviors, prejudice, and emotional volatility. By helping people address and release these influences, Scientologists believe they can contribute to a more harmonious society. A Clear Planet would have individuals who can communicate openly, resolve conflicts peacefully, and act with self-awareness, rather than being driven by unexamined fears or grudges. Scientologists see this as a foundation for a world where cooperation and understanding replace hostility and division.

**Education and outreach** are key strategies in working toward a Clear Planet. Scientologists engage in programs that aim to make the teachings and tools of Scientology accessible to anyone interested in self-improvement. Through courses, public events, and the availability of materials like *The Way to Happiness*, which offers common-sense moral guidelines, they provide people with practical approaches to improve their lives and communities. Scientologists believe that these tools are essential for achieving a society where individuals have the resources to handle their own lives effectively, which is an important step toward the vision of a Clear Planet.

In a Clear Planet, **personal responsibility and ethical conduct** would be the standard. Scientologists believe that individuals who have reached the state of Clear naturally tend to make ethical decisions because they have resolved internal conflicts that lead to harmful actions. For Scientologists, a Clear Planet would mean a world where people take responsibility not only for themselves but also for the well-being of others, acting with integrity in their personal and professional lives. This alignment with ethical values is seen as vital for creating social stability, as individuals who act responsibly contribute to a society that supports growth, understanding, and mutual respect.

The **elimination of widespread social issues** is another aspect of the Clear Planet vision. Scientologists believe that when individuals clear their minds of reactive influences, they are less likely to engage in destructive behaviors like substance abuse, crime, or violence. By helping individuals achieve a Clear state, Scientologists aim to reduce the root causes of these issues. A Clear Planet, therefore, represents a world where individuals are self-sufficient, mentally clear, and capable of making decisions that benefit themselves and others. In this vision, social issues would diminish, creating a society focused on constructive goals and personal development.

Scientologists also see a Clear Planet as **a place of spiritual growth and progress**. Beyond the state of Clear, Scientology offers higher levels on the Bridge, where individuals can explore their full potential as spiritual beings, known as Operating Thetans. In a Clear Planet, many people would not only have resolved their own limitations but would also work toward expanding their understanding and connection to the spiritual realm. This heightened awareness is believed to contribute to a more insightful, connected, and purpose-driven society, where individuals seek not only to better themselves but also to contribute positively to the larger human experience.

A Clear Planet represents an ideal where **communication, understanding, and compassion** form the basis of human interaction. In this vision, Scientologists see people who are not only free from the constraints of their own minds but are also equipped to support others in their journey. As more individuals reach the state of Clear, Scientologists believe the cumulative effect will be a society where people are better able to work together, appreciate differences, and support a common vision for a peaceful, thriving world.

# Growth and Expansion of Scientology

In the future, Scientology envisions significant **growth and expansion**, reaching new communities and introducing more individuals to its teachings and practices. Scientologists believe that as more people become aware of the benefits of auditing, training, and the spiritual tools offered by Scientology, the movement will continue to grow. Expansion is not solely about numbers; it's about building a global community dedicated to spiritual advancement, personal empowerment, and ethical living. Scientologists work to increase outreach through new churches, missions, and public engagement efforts that bring Scientology's philosophy to individuals across diverse cultural and social backgrounds.

One way Scientology fosters growth is by **establishing new organizations and missions** worldwide. Each Scientology organization offers a place where individuals can participate in auditing, study courses, and gain a deeper understanding of the principles of Scientology. These centers serve as local hubs where people can connect with others on similar journeys, creating communities that support spiritual growth and self-discovery. Scientologists see these missions and churches as essential for helping individuals in every part of the world access tools for personal development, creating a network that reaches even remote areas.

Scientology's expansion also includes **making its materials more accessible** through translations and international distribution. Books, courses, and audiovisual materials are translated into multiple languages, enabling individuals from various backgrounds to engage with Scientology's teachings. This accessibility allows for a global spread of ideas, ensuring that language barriers do not prevent individuals from discovering the principles of auditing, personal responsibility, and the Bridge to Total Freedom. By reaching a wider audience, Scientology aims to create a more inclusive environment that welcomes people from all cultures and encourages cross-cultural understanding and unity.

**Public awareness campaigns** are another key aspect of Scientology's growth strategy. Scientologists use educational programs, events, and social media to share information on topics like the importance of ethical living, the benefits of a drug-free lifestyle, and the basics of Scientology's spiritual practices. Campaigns such as The Way to Happiness promote values like respect, honesty, and compassion, resonating with individuals regardless of their background or beliefs. These campaigns help broaden the public's understanding of Scientology's mission and attract individuals who are looking for practical ways to improve their lives.

Scientologists see **collaborative partnerships** as a way to expand their influence and create opportunities for outreach. Partnering with schools, community organizations, and other institutions allows Scientologists to introduce programs that promote literacy, drug prevention, and human rights awareness. Through collaboration, Scientology can connect with individuals who might not have otherwise encountered its teachings, while also contributing positively to the communities they work with. These partnerships reflect Scientology's commitment to making a tangible difference in society, aligning its growth with social betterment.

# Scientology's Role in Modern Spirituality and Society

In a rapidly changing world, **Scientology positions itself as a modern spiritual path** that addresses contemporary challenges with practical solutions. Scientologists believe that their practices offer individuals tools to achieve mental clarity, personal responsibility, and spiritual awareness in a way that resonates with modern life. Unlike traditional religions, which often focus on faith and rituals, Scientology emphasizes hands-on techniques like auditing, which provide measurable personal growth and self-discovery. This approach makes Scientology relevant to individuals seeking spirituality grounded in tangible results, allowing it to meet the needs of today's society.

Scientology also promotes the concept of **personal empowerment** as central to its spiritual path. In a world where many face stress, uncertainty, and self-doubt, Scientology's teachings offer methods for overcoming these challenges. By providing individuals with the skills to confront and resolve mental barriers, Scientology positions itself as a path for those who want to take charge of their own lives. This empowerment is achieved through tools like auditing, training routines, and self-reflection, giving Scientologists a means to grow spiritually while navigating the demands of daily life.

Another aspect of Scientology's role in modern spirituality is its emphasis on **self-discovery and the nature of the thetan**, or spiritual self. In a society increasingly interested in exploring consciousness and spiritual awareness, Scientology's teachings on the thetan resonate with those seeking answers beyond the material world. Scientologists believe that by understanding their spiritual nature, they can achieve greater purpose and connection to life's meaning. This concept appeals to individuals who want to explore spirituality without the traditional limitations of doctrine, offering an alternative path focused on self-knowledge and spiritual freedom.

Scientology's **commitment to social betterment** also aligns with its place in modern society. By focusing on programs that address issues like literacy, drug addiction, and human rights, Scientology aims to improve the quality of life in communities around the world. Scientologists believe that spirituality includes ethical responsibility and that each individual can contribute positively to society. Through outreach initiatives, Scientology offers support to those struggling with societal challenges, reinforcing the idea that spiritual development and social well-being are interconnected.

Scientology provides a path that **embraces the integration of spirituality and practical tools** for self-improvement. By combining spiritual insight with actionable techniques, Scientology offers individuals a modern approach to personal development that encourages self-responsibility and ethical living. As society evolves and people search for ways to manage complex emotional and psychological challenges, Scientology's methods present a distinctive approach that aims to harmonize personal growth with spiritual exploration, making it increasingly relevant to contemporary seekers.

# Adaptation to Technological and Cultural Changes

As society evolves, **Scientology adapts to technological and cultural shifts** to stay relevant and accessible to individuals around the world. Scientologists recognize that technology has transformed how people communicate, learn, and access information, and they strive to leverage these advancements to support their mission. By using modern tools like digital platforms, online courses, and virtual outreach programs, Scientology reaches individuals who might not have physical access to a local church or mission. These adaptations allow Scientology to engage with a global audience, providing resources that fit the needs of modern learners and creating new ways for people to connect with its teachings.

One way Scientology adapts is by **offering online resources** that allow people to study Scientology materials, participate in courses, and connect with others remotely. This approach broadens access to the Bridge to Total Freedom, allowing individuals to progress at their own pace, regardless of their location. Through online courses and digital materials, Scientologists can study and apply the teachings from wherever they are, bringing a sense of flexibility and convenience to the process. This accessibility reflects Scientology's commitment to making spiritual growth available to as many people as possible, even in a digitally connected world.

Scientology also adapts by using **multimedia to enhance learning**. Audiovisual materials, interactive courses, and virtual seminars are used to present Scientology concepts in engaging, accessible formats. By combining traditional study methods with modern media, Scientology aims to make its teachings easier to understand and apply, particularly for younger generations who are accustomed to digital content. This multimedia approach aligns with the way people consume information today, helping Scientologists engage more effectively with current and future members.

The organization has also embraced social media and digital outreach as a way to **promote Scientology's social programs and ethical teachings**. Platforms like YouTube, Twitter, and Instagram allow Scientologists to share information on topics like drug prevention, human rights, and personal ethics with a broad audience. These platforms provide an opportunity to dispel misconceptions, answer questions, and offer insights into Scientology's purpose and programs. By engaging actively on social media, Scientology can maintain an open line of communication with the public, presenting its message in a way that aligns with modern culture and preferences for transparency.

As **cultural attitudes shift**, Scientology remains adaptable in how it communicates its message of self-responsibility, ethical conduct, and spiritual awareness. In an increasingly diverse society, Scientology embraces inclusivity by making its teachings applicable to people of all backgrounds. Scientologists believe that their practices can benefit anyone interested in self-improvement, regardless of cultural or religious beliefs. By maintaining an inclusive approach and adapting its outreach to resonate with different audiences, Scientology works to stay relevant across cultural lines, positioning itself as a universal path to personal and spiritual growth.

Scientology's adaptations to technological and cultural changes include a focus on **privacy and data security**, particularly in the digital age. As auditing and personal progress are deeply personal, Scientologists take steps to ensure that individuals' information and experiences remain confidential. Adapting to new privacy standards, Scientology uses secure platforms and data protection measures to honor this commitment to confidentiality. This approach builds trust with new and current members, demonstrating that Scientology prioritizes the privacy and integrity of each individual's spiritual journey.

Through these adaptations, Scientology remains focused on **staying accessible, relevant, and supportive** of individuals in an ever-evolving world. By embracing technology and aligning with cultural developments, Scientology aims to create a future where its teachings and tools are available to anyone seeking personal growth and spiritual exploration. This adaptability ensures that Scientology's vision of a Clear Planet remains achievable, meeting the needs of a changing society while staying true to its core principles.

# APPENDIX

## Terms and Definitions

- **Scientology**: A modern religion founded by L. Ron Hubbard, focusing on personal growth and spiritual awareness.
- **Dianetics**: A methodology developed by Hubbard for addressing the reactive mind to achieve mental clarity and freedom.
- **Thetan**: The true spiritual self of an individual, considered immortal and separate from the body and mind.
- **Auditing**: A counseling process in Scientology where an individual explores past experiences to release mental barriers.
- **E-Meter**: A device used in auditing to measure the mental state or changes in energy of an individual, aiding in identifying engrams.
- **Clear**: A state achieved through auditing where an individual is free from the reactive mind's influence.
- **Reactive Mind**: The part of the mind that stores painful or traumatic memories, called engrams, which can affect behavior.
- **Analytical Mind**: The rational, conscious part of the mind that makes decisions based on reason and observation.
- **Engram**: A memory of a painful or traumatic experience stored in the reactive mind.
- **Operating Thetan (OT)**: Advanced spiritual levels in Scientology, where an individual gains increasing awareness and control over their spiritual existence.
- **Bridge to Total Freedom**: The structured path in Scientology that guides individuals from pre-Clear to Clear and through the OT levels.
- **ARC Triangle**: A concept representing Affinity, Reality, and Communication, three elements essential to understanding and relationships.
- **KRC Triangle**: The triangle representing Knowledge, Responsibility, and Control, crucial for personal empowerment.
- **Eight Dynamics**: The levels or urges of life's survival, ranging from the individual to the universe or infinity.
- **First Dynamic**: The urge to survive as oneself; the self.
- **Second Dynamic**: The urge to survive through family and procreation.
- **Third Dynamic**: The urge to survive as part of a group or community.
- **Fourth Dynamic**: The urge to survive as humankind.
- **Fifth Dynamic**: The urge to survive through life forms, including plants and animals.
- **Sixth Dynamic**: The urge to survive within the physical universe, including matter, energy, space, and time.
- **Seventh Dynamic**: The urge to survive as a spiritual being.
- **Eighth Dynamic**: The urge to survive as part of the infinite or Supreme Being.
- **Training Routines (TRs)**: Exercises to improve concentration, communication, and control over one's reactions.

- **Overt**: A harmful or unethical act against another, self, or society.
- **Withhold**: The act of holding back an overt, creating guilt and lowering awareness.
- **ARC Break**: A sudden disruption in Affinity, Reality, or Communication, causing upset or disconnection.
- **Org**: Short for "organization," a Scientology church or mission.
- **Mission**: A smaller Scientology church that offers introductory courses and services.
- **Org Board**: The organizational chart or structure of a Scientology organization, delineating roles and responsibilities.
- **HCO (Hubbard Communications Office)**: The division responsible for communication and administration within a Scientology organization.
- **Sea Org (Sea Organization)**: An elite group within Scientology, dedicated to serving the church full-time.
- **Fair Game**: A term historically used to describe handling or neutralizing opponents of Scientology.
- **PTS (Potential Trouble Source)**: A person connected to a suppressive person, often resulting in personal difficulties or instability.
- **Suppressive Person (SP)**: An individual deemed harmful or antagonistic to Scientology, often disconnected from to prevent negative influence.
- **Disconnection**: The practice of severing ties with a person deemed suppressive or a source of negative influence.
- **Code of Honor**: A set of ethical principles followed by Scientologists to guide behavior and decision-making.
- **The Way to Happiness**: A moral code written by Hubbard containing 21 principles for ethical and constructive living.
- **Purification Rundown**: A program designed to detoxify the body through exercise, sauna, and vitamins, improving physical and spiritual health.
- **Narconon**: A Scientology-based drug rehabilitation program aiming to help individuals overcome addiction.
- **Applied Scholastics**: An organization promoting Hubbard's Study Technology for effective learning.
- **Study Technology**: A method developed by Hubbard to improve comprehension and retention of knowledge, focusing on barriers to learning.
- **The Tone Scale**: A chart showing a range of emotions or states of mind, used to understand behavior and improve communication.
- **Ethics Conditions**: Levels of ethics applied to situations in life, used to improve conditions through specified actions.
- **PTS/SP Course**: A course that teaches Scientologists to identify and handle suppressive influences in their lives.
- **Fair Game Policy**: A policy regarding how Scientology handled critics and opponents, now claimed to be discontinued.
- **Knowledge Report**: A report written by a Scientologist to document unethical or harmful behavior observed in others.
- **Field Staff Member (FSM)**: A Scientologist who helps introduce others to Scientology services and materials.
- **Case**: A term used to describe an individual's mental and spiritual condition or difficulties.

- **Case Supervisor**: A trained Scientologist who oversees auditing processes and guides progress.
- **Process**: An auditing technique or question used to guide an individual in exploring and resolving specific issues.
- **PC (Preclear)**: An individual who has not yet achieved Clear and is receiving auditing.
- **Tone 40**: A high state of intention on the Tone Scale, representing absolute certainty and command.
- **Tech (Technology)**: Refers to Hubbard's techniques and methods in Scientology for spiritual development.
- **L. Ron Hubbard**: The founder of Scientology and author of numerous books and courses on spiritual and personal improvement.
- **Tech Dictionary**: A glossary used by Scientologists containing terms and definitions for studying Scientology materials.
- **Auditor's Code**: Guidelines followed by auditors to ensure ethical and supportive conduct during auditing sessions.
- **Postulate**: A decision or intention that can affect one's reality, often a positive affirmation of a goal.
- **Help Factor**: A measure of one's willingness to help others, important in understanding relationships in Scientology.
- **Command Intention**: A directive or goal set by the church's leadership to guide organizational efforts and activities.
- **Flag**: Scientology's international headquarters located in Clearwater, Florida, which offers advanced spiritual services.
- **Golden Age of Tech**: A series of initiatives to refine and standardize Scientology's training and auditing methods.
- **LRH**: Abbreviation for L. Ron Hubbard, used frequently in Scientology materials.
- **Fair Use Doctrine**: A legal principle that Scientologists sometimes invoke when handling public materials or criticism.
- **Tone 4.0**: An ideal level on the Tone Scale, representing enthusiasm and a positive outlook.
- **Qual (Qualifications)**: The department within a Scientology organization responsible for maintaining and improving standards.
- **Release**: A state attained in auditing where an individual has relief from specific mental barriers or issues.
- **PTS Type A and Type B**: Categories of Potential Trouble Sources, Type A being someone connected to a suppressive person and Type B being under active suppression.
- **Suppress**: To stop or hinder, particularly referring to influences or people that inhibit spiritual growth in Scientology.

# AFTERWORD

Thank you for taking the time to consider *Scientology Step by Step – Understanding the Beliefs, Practices & Goals of Scientology*. I hope this book has helped demystify Scientology, giving you a clear, balanced view of its beliefs, practices, and vision for personal and spiritual growth.

Throughout these pages, we've explored the fundamental ideas and core practices that define Scientology. From the concept of the Thetan and the role of the mind, to the structured path of the Bridge to Total Freedom, and the importance of ethics, auditing, and personal responsibility, you've now seen what Scientology means to those who practice it. More than just a collection of beliefs, Scientology is a framework for self-discovery, improvement, and a commitment to enhancing life in a meaningful way. It offers its followers tools to examine their lives, resolve personal struggles, and strive toward a state of freedom and fulfillment.

Along the way, we also discussed how Scientology engages with broader society, from community outreach programs to social initiatives, all driven by the belief that positive change in individuals can inspire positive change in the world. Scientology's goal to contribute to a peaceful, ethical society is one that resonates with many, even beyond the Church. This ambition reflects a vision of spirituality that seeks to create real, lasting impact—starting with the self and extending outward.

Whether you've read this book out of personal curiosity, an academic interest, or a deeper desire to understand Scientology's role in the modern world, I hope it has given you a fair and insightful perspective. Learning about any belief system, especially one as intricate as Scientology, is a reminder of the variety of ways people search for meaning, peace, and purpose.

As with any spiritual or philosophical path, Scientology is a personal journey, and understanding it fully requires more than just reading—it requires openness, reflection, and sometimes, asking challenging questions. But whatever your own perspective or background, I hope this book has broadened your understanding and given you something valuable to think about.

Thank you for allowing me to guide you through Scientology, step by step. May this exploration serve as a reminder that there are many paths to understanding ourselves, each one offering unique insights and opportunities for growth. And as you go forward, may your own journey be filled with curiosity, learning, and inspiration.

Made in the USA
Las Vegas, NV
13 February 2025

18124145R00079